Chef Dez
Cooks
with BC Eggs

ANOTHER GREAT
COOKBOOK FROM
CHEF, WRITER, & HOST:
CHEF DEZ

DEDICATION

To Amanda

Thank you for your faith and trust in me.

CONTENTS

FOREWORD

BC Egg is pleased to partner with Chef Dez on an egg-focused cookbook. Obviously, we're biased, but we think eggs are the perfect food! Not only are they nutritious powerhouses with 6.5 grams of protein per egg, all nine essential amino acids and 14 other key nutrients (and only 80 calories per egg) but they are so versatile. You can eat eggs for breakfast, brunch, lunch, dinner, dessert and for a snack. The recipes in this book will help you find new ways to eat eggs and you might discover a new favourite.

BC has 149* egg farms. Each farm is family owned and operated. The average flock size in BC is 22,000 hens and we have several ways of raising hens. While old-style conventional cages are being phased out, newer enriched cages offer hens twice the space along with perches, nest boxes and scratch areas. Free-run barns allow the hens to roam freely about the inside of the barn in order to access perches, nest boxes and a scratch area. Free-range barns are similar to free-run barns, but they also offer the hens the opportunity to go outside. BC is the only province to regulate how much time the hens must be given access to the outdoors – 120 days a year and a minimum of six hours per day. Organic barns are very similar to free-range ones, but the birds have a bit more space both inside and outside as well as being fed a certified organic diet.

No matter what type of egg you buy, they are all nutritionally equivalent. In addition, hens are well cared for by their farmer regardless of what type of barn they live in.

If you want to learn more about how hens are raised in BC – and meet some egg farmers – please visit our website at www.bcegg.com.

Amanda Brittain
Director of Communications and Marketing
BC Egg

*As at the publication date of this book.

SPREADS, DIPS, & SAUCES

Aioli

"Simple garlic mayonnaise"

1 large egg
1/2 cup oil
A squeeze of lemon juice
1 garlic clove, minced
Salt to taste

1. Add all ingredients to a blender carafe or hand-blender carafe and blend together until fully emulsified, smooth, and thickened. Can be refrigerated in a clean, air-tight container for up to one week.

Chipotle Aioli

Recipe Courtesy of BC Egg, bcegg.com
"Homemade mayonnaise with a kick!"

3 egg yolks
2 garlic cloves, sliced
1 teaspoon lemon juice
1/2 teaspoon salt
1 tablespoon canned chipotle peppers in adobo sauce
1 cup canola oil or vegetable oil

1. In a food processor, combine the egg yolks, garlic, lemon juice, salt, and the chipotle peppers in adobo sauce.
2. Turn the food processor on high and very slowly drizzle in the oil. The aioli will become smooth after about a minute and will start to resemble a mayonnaise. Refrigerate until ready to serve.

Hollandaise Sauce

Recipe Courtesy of BC Egg, bcegg.com

"Not just for Eggs Benedict, Hollandaise sauce is delicious drizzled over many seafood and vegetable dishes including salmon and asparagus. Try making it in the microwave, on the stovetop, or even in the blender."

3 egg yolks
1 tablespoon lemon juice
Pinch of ground cayenne pepper or dry mustard
Pinch of salt
1/2 cup butter, melted

1. Whisk egg yolks in glass or stainless-steel bowl until frothy. Whisk in lemon juice, cayenne pepper and salt.
2. Set bowl over a saucepan containing about 1.5 inches of simmering water (bottom of bowl should not touch the water). Heat, whisking constantly, until egg mixture turns pale yellow, thickens slightly, and increases in volume. Remove from heat. Slowly whisk in melted butter until sauce is smooth and thickened. Serve warm.

Makes approximately 3/4 cup

NOTES

MICROWAVE METHOD: Whisk egg yolks, lemon juice, cayenne pepper and salt in 4-cup (1 L) glass measuring cup until blended. Slowly whisk in melted butter. Microwave on Medium (50% power) until sauce thickens, 45 seconds to 1 minute. Whisk after 30 seconds and at end of cooking to produce a smooth sauce.

BLENDER METHOD: Process egg yolks, lemon juice, cayenne pepper and salt in blender just until smooth. With blender running, slowly add melted butter, processing until thickened and fluffy.

Curdling may occur due to overbeating or adding butter too quickly. To rescue a curdled sauce, try one of the following:

Whisk another egg yolk in a small bowl. Gradually whisk yolk into the curdled Hollandaise Sauce.

Place 1 tablespoon water in a medium bowl. Whisk a small amount of separated sauce into water until it becomes smooth. Keep adding sauce slowly, while continuing to whisk vigorously.

Béarnaise Sauce

In the previous Hollandaise Sauce recipe, replace the lemon juice with tarragon vinegar and add 1 tablespoon chopped fresh parsley and 1/2 teaspoon dried tarragon leaves.

Mayonnaise

Recipe Courtesy of BC Egg, bcegg.com

2 egg yolks
1 teaspoon Dijon mustard
2 teaspoons lemon juice or white vinegar
1 cup vegetable oil
Salt and pepper to taste

1. Add eggs, mustard, and lemon juice or vinegar to a blender and pulse till combined.
2. With the blender running, slowly add oil in a thin stream. Blend on high till fully emulsified, thick, and creamy. Season to taste with salt and pepper.

NOTES

Can be refrigerated in a clean, air-tight container for up to one week.

If the mayonnaise separates, it can be saved by adding one egg yolk and a teaspoon of warm water while whisking CONSTANTLY. Finish by VERY slowly and gradually whisking in another 1/4 cup of oil.

APPETIZERS

Guacamole Devilled Eggs

Recipe Courtesy of BC Egg, bcegg.com

8-10 large eggs, hard boiled
2 medium ripe (soft) avocados
2 tablespoons fresh lime juice
1/2 cup minced onion
2 tablespoons chopped fresh cilantro
1 tablespoon garlic powder
1 cup diced tomato
Salt and fresh ground pepper, to taste
Pinch of Mexican chilli powder, for garnish
Tortilla chips, for garnish
Cilantro leaves, for garnish

1. Crack and peel the BC Eggs, then halve the eggs. Remove yolks and put them into mixing bowl. Set aside the halved egg whites.
2. To the egg yolks, add the avocado, lime juice, onion, cilantro, and garlic powder. Mash and mix until thoroughly combined. Stir in the diced tomato and season to taste with salt & pepper.
3. Spoon the mixture into the reserved egg white halves.
4. Garnish each one with a sprinkle of chilli powder, 1 tortilla chip, and 1 cilantro leaf. Serve immediately.

Makes 16 to 20

Bacon Fritters

Recipe Courtesy of BC Egg, bcegg.com

"Best served with the Chipotle Aioli in the Spreads, Dips & Sauces Chapter"

4 slices bacon, chopped finely
2 ears fresh corn
1/2 cup butter
1 cup milk
1/2 teaspoon salt
1 teaspoon white sugar
3 dashes Tabasco sauce
1.25 cups all-purpose flour
4 large eggs
3/4 cup grated aged white Cheddar cheese
2 tablespoons finely chopped fresh parsley
1/4 teaspoon freshly ground black pepper
4 cups canola or vegetable oil (for frying)

1. In a non-stick pan over medium heat, fry the bacon pieces until fully cooked and crispy. Set aside with a slotted spoon.
2. Cut the kernels off the ears of corn and fry in the residual bacon fat over medium heat until light toasty brown in spots. Set aside.
3. Place the butter, milk, salt, sugar, and Tabasco in a pot and bring to simmer. Add the flour and stir well. Cook the mixture over a low heat, stirring continuously, when it clumps around the spoon, transfer to a stand mixer. Mix the batter on a medium/low setting for a couple of minutes to allow it to cool slightly.
4. Crack the eggs into a small bowl. With the mixer on medium speed, add one egg and mix until it incorporates into the flour mixture. Add the second egg and beat until the batter looks smooth. Repeat two more times until the batter has absorbed the eggs, appears lighter and is clinging to the sides of the bowl again.
5. Add the reserved cooked bacon pieces, reserved cooked kernels of corn, grated Cheddar cheese, parsley, and pepper. Fold everything

together until well combined and chill the batter in the refrigerator until it firms up.

6. When ready to cook the fritters, heat the canola oil until it reaches 350°F to 375°F. Using two tablespoons, drop little balls of the batter carefully into the oil. Work in batches, to avoid crowding your pot. Fry until golden brown and the fritters are floating, about 5 minutes.

7. Remove from the oil and rest on a plate lined with paper towel to absorb any extra oil. Serve warm with chipotle aioli.

Makes approximately 24 fritters

Scotch Eggs
"A classic and popular Scottish appetizer... or great as a snack or breakfast too!"

1 cup soda cracker crumbs
1/2 cup minced fresh parsley
6 large hard-boiled eggs
680g (1.5 pounds) pork breakfast sausages

1. Preheat oven to 375°F.
2. Mix the cracker crumbs and the parsley together in a shallow dish.
3. Peel the eggs. Squeeze the sausage meat from the casings and discard the casings. Encase each of the peeled eggs in an equal amount of the sausage meat.
4. Roll each of the sausage coated eggs in the crumb/parsley mixture. Place on a baking sheet and bake for 30-35 minutes until the sausage meat is cooked through, turning occasionally.
5. Store in refrigerator until ready to serve. Cut each egg into 4 wedges for serving.

Makes 24 wedges

Chinese Take-Out Egg Rolls

"You can use either Egg Roll Wrappers or Spring Roll Wrappers for this recipe. I prefer the Spring Roll Wrappers as they are thinner, come out crispier, and are more like the egg rolls you get with Chinese Take-Out. A standard sized cheese grater will make quick work out of most of your prep for this recipe. An oil thermometer is a must for this recipe."

100g (3.5oz) vermicelli rice noodles*
454g (1 pound) lean ground pork
2 teaspoons canola or vegetable oil
3 teaspoons salt, separated
1 teaspoon pepper
2 teaspoons Chinese 5-spice powder, separated
2 packed cups grated cabbage
1 medium/large carrot, grated, approximately 1 packed cup
1 small onion, grated, approximately 1/2 packed cup
6 garlic cloves, finely minced or crushed to a paste
3 tablespoons grated fresh ginger
2 tablespoons soy sauce
2 tablespoons oyster sauce
1 tablespoon sesame oil
2 eggs, beaten
Canola oil for frying
454g (1 pound) package of fresh spring roll wrappers (8x8 inches in size)
-or-
2 – 454g packages of fresh egg roll wrappers (5x5 inches in size)

1. Put vermicelli noodles in a stainless-steel bowl and pour boiling water over them. Separate with a fork and let stand for 5 minutes. Then drain in wire mesh strainer and rinse with cold water. Let stand draining while you continue with the recipe.
2. In a large pan over medium-high heat, add the pork, 2 teaspoons canola oil, 2 teaspoons of the salt, pepper, and 1 teaspoon of the 5-spice powder. Cook, stirring frequently, until browned and a little crispy, about 7-10 minutes. Remove with a slotted spoon and set aside in a large bowl.

3. Turn the heat to medium and add the cabbage, carrot, onion, garlic, ginger, soy sauce, the last 1 teaspoon of the salt, and the other 1 teaspoon of the 5-spice powder. Cook, stirring occasionally, until tender, about 6-8 minutes. Transfer this cabbage mixture to the large bowl with the pork. Stir in the oyster sauce and sesame oil.

4. Place the drained vermicelli noodles on a cutting board and cut into small pieces (about 1 inch) and mix into pork/cabbage mixture to complete the filling. This will be approximately 6 cups of filling.

5. Separate your wrappers. If using the larger spring roll wrappers you will use 1/3 cup filling per wrapper. If using the smaller egg roll wrappers you will use 3-4 tablespoons of filling per wrapper. Place the wrapper with 1 point facing you (looks like a diamond). Place 1 portion of the filling just below the center of the wrapper. Brush the top 2 edges with some beaten egg. Wrap the bottom point of the wrapper over the filling, tuck the side points of the wrapper over the filling, and then roll away from you to seal the egg roll (make sure that the filling is fairly tightly encased with the wrap as you roll to make a good seal). Continue until all filling is used (you will have some leftover wrappers). Set these wrapped egg rolls on a tray.

6. In a large deep pot, add enough canola oil for about a 2 to 3 inch depth of oil. Heat the oil until you can maintain a consistent temperature of 350 to 375 degrees Fahrenheit.

7. Working in batches, carefully place 3 to 4 rolls in the hot oil, one at a time. Fry until golden brown and crispy: 3 minutes for spring roll wrappers, and approximately 4 to 5 minutes for egg roll wrappers. Set aside on a wire rack when done.

8. Repeat previous step until all the rolls are cooked. Serve with your favorite plum sauce and enjoy!

Makes 18 rolls if you use spring roll wrappers, or 24 rolls with egg roll wrappers

*Vermicelli rice noodles can be found in the Asian/Import aisle of most major grocery stores

Fig & Balsamic Vegetable Tart

Balsamic Glaze
1/2 cup balsamic vinegar
2 tablespoons dark brown sugar

Put the balsamic vinegar and brown sugar in a small pot. Bring to a boil over medium heat and continue to cook uncovered until reduced to half the volume (1/4 cup), approximately 10 minutes. Remove from the pot and set aside.

1 small zucchini
1/4 cup oil packed sliced sun-dried tomatoes, drained, tomatoes & oil reserved separately
Salt & pepper
454g (1pound) package thawed puff pastry, chilled
All-purpose flour for dusting
2 large eggs, divided
1/2 cup sour cream
5 tablespoons soft unripened goat cheese, divided
1 teaspoon dried basil
1 garlic clove, minced
1/2 teaspoon salt
1/4 teaspoon ground black pepper
8 small dried dark figs, quartered
Handful of fresh arugula greens
Handful of grape tomatoes, sliced into circles
2 to 3 tablespoons of balsamic glaze (from above)
Fresh cracked pepper

1. Preheat your oven to 425°F (400°F convection) and line a baking sheet with parchment paper.
2. Slice the zucchini lengthwise into 1/4-inch strips. Brush these strips with the reserved oil from the sundried tomatoes and season with salt and pepper. Grill these strips over a medium-high flame, or a medium

hot grill pan, until grill marks appear. Remove from the heat and set aside.

3. Remove the thawed puff pastry from the fridge. Using a minimal amount of flour, roll out the puff pastry into a rectangle approximately 11 by 16 inches, about 1/4 inch thick. Transfer to the prepared baking sheet and make an edge by folding over 3/4 inch of the pastry around all 4 sides. Using a fork, dock the pastry (not the edges though, just the inside part) about every inch.

4. Beat 1 of the eggs. Using a pastry brush, brush the formed edges of the pastry until coated, and then put the leftover part of this beaten egg in a mixing bowl. To that mixing bowl add the other egg, sour cream, 2 tablespoons of the goat cheese, basil, garlic, 1/2 teaspoon salt, and 1/4 teaspoon pepper. Mix thoroughly until combined. Pour this mixture onto the docked pastry keeping inside the formed edges.

5. Arrange the prepared zucchini slices and on the egg/sour cream filling. Bake until the pastry is puffed up and golden brown, approximately 20 minutes. Remove from the oven and let cool 10 minutes.

6. Sprinkle the top of the cooked/cooled tart with the reserved sun-dried tomato slices, quartered figs, the remaining 3 tablespoons of crumbled goat cheese, arugula greens, and grape tomato slices. Drizzle 2 to 3 tablespoons of the balsamic glaze over the tart along with many grinds of fresh cracked pepper. Cut into 12 portions and serve immediately.

Makes 12 portions

 Every large egg has 6.5 grams of protein, all 9 essential amino acids, and 14 key nutrients that help maintain healthy bones, teeth, skin and eyes. All for only 80 calories!

Jack O' Lantern Devilled Eggs – Makes 12 halves

"Time to have a little fun with your eggs this Halloween! Don't fuss too much with these as each one should be unique. Adding a little butter to the egg yolk mixture helps the filling hold up better."

6 large hard-boiled eggs, peeled
Paprika for sprinkling
2 tablespoons mayonnaise
1 tablespoon room temperature butter
1 tablespoon Dijon mustard
1 tablespoon sweet green relish
2 teaspoons red wine vinegar
1/2 teaspoon sugar
1/4 teaspoon Worcestershire sauce
1/4 teaspoon salt
1/8 teaspoon pepper
Skin from 1 cucumber

1. Carefully cut the eggs in half lengthwise. Remove the yolks and place them in a small mixing bowl.
2. Sprinkle some paprika over the cut side of the egg whites.
3. To the reserved egg yolks, and the mayonnaise, butter, mustard, relish, vinegar, sugar, Worcestershire, salt and pepper. Mash until smooth. Spoon this mixture into a disposable sandwich bag and then cut the corner off to make a piping bag. Carefully pipe this mixture equally into the hollowed egg whites. Chill in the refrigerator during the next step.
4. Using a vegetable peeler, take long strips of skin off a cucumber. Cut the dark green skin strips into many small triangles to decorate as the eyes and noses. Use a small round cookie cutter (a fluted edge one works best) to make semi-circle shapes to decorate as mouths. Decorate the filling in the egg whites with the cucumber skin eyes, noses, and mouths (the pointed tip of a small knife will be helpful in carefully placing the face decorations, or a sanitized pair of tweezers).
5. Arrange on a platter and serve immediately or refrigerate until needed.

RECIPE NOTES

South-Western Corn Fritters

"Less batter than a pancake, and lots of corn. If you don't have fresh corn, then use thawed frozen corn that has been patted dry really well, and then measure the 1.5 cups."

1.5 cups fresh corn kernels
1/4 cup small diced red bell pepper
1/2 jalapeno, minced (seeds & white membrane removed first)
2 teaspoons minced chives
2/3 cup all-purpose flour
4 teaspoons cornstarch
1 teaspoon salt
1/2 teaspoon pepper
2 large eggs, beaten
3 tablespoons milk
1/2 cup canola oil, for frying

Chipotle Sauce

1/2 cup mayonnaise
2 teaspoons liquid honey
1.5 teaspoons minced chipotle peppers (from a can)
1 teaspoon lime juice
1/4 teaspoon salt

1. Combine the corn kernels, bell pepper, jalapeno, and chives in a medium size mixing bowl. Add the flour, cornstarch, 1 teaspoon salt, pepper, eggs, and milk. Stir to combine to make a chunky batter.
2. In a separate small bowl, combine the mayonnaise, honey, chipotle, lime juice, and 1/4 teaspoon salt. Set aside.
3. Heat a 10" skillet (I prefer cast iron because it holds heat so well) over medium heat. Add the oil and heat the oil for about 5 minutes until hot. You can test the oil by putting a very small amount of the mixture (about 1/2 teaspoon) and you should hear it sizzling.
4. Take a standard size soup spoon and carefully put 4 heaping spoonfuls of the batter into the hot oil, in four spots. Fry until golden brown on the one side, before turning them over to brown the other side. Should

be approximately 3 minutes per side, but the golden-brown exterior is your goal. The time is just for approximation.

5. Transfer the four cooked fritters to drain on paper towel.
6. Repeat steps #4 and #5 to make 12 fritters total. Let cool slightly before serving with the chipotle sauce.

Makes 12 corn fritters (each approximately 2 to 3 inches in size)

Tomato & Corn Galette

"Tomatoes, corn, and goat cheese embraced by pie pastry is so deliciously good"

<u>Filling</u>
150g soft unripened goat cheese
6 large fresh basil leaves, sliced thin
1 large egg
1/2 teaspoon salt
1/4 teaspoon ground black pepper

1/4 cup sliced oil packed sun-dried tomatoes, drained and oil reserved
1.5 cups grape tomato halves (sliced lengthwise)
1 tablespoon balsamic vinegar
1 unbaked pie shell
1/2 cup fresh corn kernels (or 1/2 cup thawed from frozen) *
1 large egg
2 teaspoons milk
1/4 cup finely grated Parmigiano-Reggiano cheese
Flaky sea salt
Fresh cracked black pepper

1. Preheat oven to 400°F convection, or 425°F conventional.
2. In a small bowl, combine the goat cheese, cut basil, 1 large egg, 1/2 teaspoon salt, and 1/4 teaspoon pepper together and set aside.
3. In a separate bowl, toss the reserved oil from the sun-dried tomatoes (keeping the sun-dried tomatoes aside) with the cut grape tomatoes and balsamic vinegar. Heat a 10-inch non-stick pan over medium-high heat. Add this tomato mixture to the pan and cook until most of the moisture in the pan is gone, approximately 3 to 4 minutes, stirring occasionally. Transfer this tomato mixture from the pan back to the bowl and set aside.
4. Roll the pie pastry to an approximate 12-to-13-inch diameter and transfer to a baking sheet. Carefully spread the reserved goat cheese mixture (from step 2) in the center while leaving about 1.5 inches of pastry all around the edge uncovered.

5. Arrange the corn kernels and reserved sliced sun-dried tomatoes on this goat cheese mixture, and then spoon on the reserved cooked tomato mixture (from step 3).
6. Fold up the edges of the pastry over just the edge of the tomatoes, pleating the pastry as necessary (for presentation). Beat 1 large egg with 2 teaspoons of milk and brush this egg wash over the folded edge of the pastry (reserve the leftover egg wash for another application such as an omelet, scrambled eggs, etc.). Sprinkle the pastry and tomatoes with the grated cheese, flaky sea salt and fresh cracked black pepper. Bake for approximately 30 to 35 minutes until the pastry is golden brown on the edges and underneath.
7. Let cool to almost room temperature before cutting into wedges and serving.

Makes 6 servings

*Tip: Reserve a few corn kernels for garnish when it comes out of the oven

<u>RECIPE NOTES</u>

SALADS & SOUPS

Greek Lemon Soup (Avgolemono)

A very authentic version of this classic Greek soup. The name of this soup is Avgolemono from the ingredients eggs (avgo) and lemon juice (lemoni).

8 cups chicken broth
1 cup long grain rice
1/2 teaspoon salt
4 large eggs
3/4 cup fresh lemon juice (approximately 4-5 large lemons)
1 teaspoon sugar
Reserved zest from lemons
Chopped fresh parsley

1. In a large saucepan or pot over high heat, bring the chicken broth to a boil.
2. Stir in the rice and the salt. Cover, reduce the heat to low and simmer for 20 minutes.
3. Separate the egg yolks from the egg whites.
4. About 5 minutes before the rice is done cooking in the broth, beat the yolks together in a small bowl, while in a large separate bowl whisk the egg whites until stiff peaks have formed. Slowly beat the mixed yolks into the whites. Then gradually beat the lemon juice into this egg mixture.
5. Gradually add 2 cups of the hot broth/rice mixture into the egg/juice mixture while whisking continuously. If the hot stock is added too fast, the eggs will curdle.
6. Once the 2 cups of broth have been added, stir the egg mixture into the large saucepan with the remaining broth/rice. Season with 1 teaspoon of sugar and serve immediately, garnished with the lemon zest and a small amount of chopped parsley.

Makes approximately 10.5 cups

Blueberry Cobb Salad

"To celebrate British Columbia's 150ᵗʰ Birthday, I wrote this version of cobb salad with ingredients that are the same colours as our BC flag – Blue, Red, Yellow, and White."

Dressing

5 strips of bacon, cut into small pieces
1 clove of garlic
1/4 cup red wine vinegar
1 tablespoon lemon juice
1 tablespoon white sugar
1 teaspoon Worcestershire sauce
1 teaspoon salt
1/2 teaspoon ground black pepper
1/4 teaspoon dry ground mustard
1/2 cup extra virgin olive oil

1. Cook the bacon in a frying pan until crisp. Reserve the rendered fat.
2. Place the bacon and the garlic in a food processor and process until minced.
3. Add the reserved bacon fat to the food processor along with all of the remaining ingredients, except for the extra virgin olive oil. Puree on high speed.
4. With the food processor still on high speed, slowly add the olive oil until thoroughly combined. Makes approximately 1 cup of dressing.

Salad

2 large romaine hearts
2 cups fresh blueberries
1 cup drained canned corn kernels
1 red bell pepper, cut into thin 1-inch strips, approx. 1 cup
1 cup crumbled mild blue cheese ~or~ 1 cup crumbled feta cheese
1 cup quartered cherry tomatoes
3 hard boiled eggs, peeled, quartered, and cut into small chunks

1. Cut the romaine hearts into small bite size pieces. Wash thoroughly and spin dry in a salad spinner. If the romaine is too wet, it will water-

down the taste of the dressing. Place on a large deep serving platter that will be big enough for tossing before serving. The romaine should be placed evenly across the platter (not mounded up).

2. By the time you have finished assembling the salad, you should have seven equal strips of ingredients covering the romaine lettuce. Start with first putting two strips of blueberries (1 cup for each strip) on each end of the pile of lettuce.

3. Then working left to right (from one strip of blueberries to the other) place the remaining ingredients in equal sized strips on the romaine lettuce: corn, red pepper, blue cheese, tomatoes, and eggs. You are now finished assembling the salad and the romaine lettuce should be completely covered with seven strips of ingredients that are the same colour as the BC Flag. Bring to the table to display with the vinaigrette separate.

4. Just before serving, pour the dressing over the salad and toss thoroughly.

Makes approximately 4 portions as a meal, or 6 to 8 as a side dish

Caesar Salad

Recipe Courtesy of BC Egg, bcegg.com

4 anchovy fillets
2 garlic cloves
2 tablespoons fresh lemon juice
1/2 teaspoon Dijon mustard
Splash of Worcestershire sauce
2 egg yolks
1/2 cup olive oil
3 tablespoons grated parmesan (optional)
Salt and pepper to taste
2-3 romaine hearts, chopped or torn into fork-friendly pieces
Croutons
Shaved parmesan or Romano cheese
4 hard boiled eggs

1. Mince the anchovies and garlic together with a pinch of salt.
2. Whisk in the lemon juice, Dijon, Worcestershire and the egg yolks. Mix well.
3. Adding very slowly, whisk in the olive oil, stirring constantly, until all is incorporated, and the dressing is thick and glossy.
4. Whisk in 3 tablespoons grated parmesan cheese, if desired, and season to taste with salt & pepper.
5. Toss the romaine with the dressing in a large bowl, till leaves are coated. You may wish to add the dressing a bit at a time, so you don't over-dress the salad.
6. Add croutons and shaved parmesan or Romano cheese.
7. Grate hard boiled eggs into the salad. If you'd rather, you can chop the eggs, or leave them in slices, but grating gives a lovely consistency. Toss and serve immediately.

Caesar Salad Dressing

"Do not substitute whole egg for the egg yolks — egg yolks are an emulsifier that will keep this dressing from separating"

1 tablespoon fresh lemon juice
1 tablespoon white wine vinegar
1 tablespoon Dijon mustard
1 teaspoon Worcestershire sauce
2 dashes tabasco sauce
3 canned anchovies
3 crushed garlic cloves
2 egg yolks
2 tablespoon dried dill
1/2 teaspoon salt
1 cup canola oil

1. Process all of the ingredients, except for the canola oil, in a food processor.
2. With the food processor running at top speed, gradually and the oil in a very slow steady stream until fully incorporated.

Makes approximately 2 cups

RECIPE NOTES

Grilled Chicken Caesar Salad

"Making the dressing and croutons from scratch is always the best for Caesar salad, but when you add grilled chicken, it's over the top!"

Dressing
1 tablespoon fresh lemon juice
1 tablespoon white wine vinegar
1 tablespoon Dijon mustard
1 teaspoon Worcestershire sauce
2 dashes tabasco sauce
3 canned anchovies
2 to 3 garlic cloves
2 egg yolks
2 tablespoons dried dill
1/2 teaspoon salt
1 cup canola oil

Croutons
4 cups of 1/2-inch diced bread cubes
3 tablespoons olive oil
1 teaspoon dried basil
1 teaspoon dried oregano
1/2 teaspoon salt
1/4 teaspoon ground black pepper

Salad
6 boneless skinless chicken breasts
3 teaspoons canola oil
Salt & pepper
15 cups chopped Romaine lettuce
1 cup finely grated Parmigiano-Reggiano cheese, divided

1. Process the dressing ingredients, EXCEPT for the 1 cup canola oil, in a food processor. Then with the food processor running at top speed, gradually add the 1 cup canola oil in a very slow steady stream until fully incorporated and emulsified. Set dressing aside in refrigerator.

2. For the croutons: Preheat your oven to 400°F. Toss the bread cubes with the olive oil, basil, oregano, 1/2 teaspoon salt, and 1/4 teaspoon pepper in a mixing bowl. Spread on a small baking sheet and bake approximately 12 minutes total (tossing them around at the 6-minute mark) until browned and crispy. Set aside.

3. Preheat your outdoor grill over a medium to medium/high flame. Butterfly cut the chicken breasts to make them thinner and more even in thickness. Oil each chicken breast with 1/2 teaspoon of canola oil and then season with salt and pepper. Grill the chicken breasts for approximately 12 to 16 minutes (6 to 8 minutes per side) until lightly charred and cooked through (71°C or 160°F). Set aside.

4. In a large mixing bowl toss the 15 cups of chopped Romaine with the reserved dressing, the reserved croutons, and 1/2 cup of the grated Parmigiano-Reggiano. Portion into 6 large salad bowls.

5. Slice or cube the cooked chicken breasts and divide equally on top of the 6 prepared salad portions. Garnish with the remaining 1/2 cup grated Parmigiano-Reggiano and serve immediately.

Makes 6 portions

 Do you know why we refrigerate eggs? It's because we wash them. Along with dirt and manure, washing removes a protective coating naturally present on eggs. Once that coating is removed, eggs have to be refrigerated to keep them from absorbing bacteria and other contaminates through the shell.

Grilled Potato Salad

"Take a step outside of the ordinary potato salad with this grilled version"

Dressing
1 cup mayonnaise
1 cup sour cream
1/4 cup liquid honey
3 tablespoons apple cider vinegar
1 tablespoon dried dill
2 teaspoons Dijon mustard
1 teaspoon seasoning salt
1/2 teaspoon fresh ground black pepper
1/2 teaspoon celery salt
1/4 teaspoon sambal oelek*, optional

Salad
1.5kg nugget potatoes
3 tablespoons canola oil, divided
Salt & Pepper
2 large red bell peppers
1 bunch green onions
1 large red onion, sliced into thick slices
4 hard-boiled large eggs, peeled, and sliced or chopped

1. Mix dressing ingredients thoroughly together and refrigerate.
2. Steam the nugget potatoes for approximately 10 minutes only, until internal temperature of the potatoes reaches approximately 160°F. Remove from steamer and toss with 1 tablespoon of the oil. Season lightly with salt & pepper and set aside.
3. Preheat BBQ over high heat.
4. Cut peppers into large pieces and toss with 1 tablespoon of oil. Grill over high heat until charred on both sides and then place in a sealed bowl or paper bag – this will create a steaming environment that will help to loosen the skins on the pepper pieces.

5. Toss the green onions in the residual oil from doing the red peppers and grill over high heat until slightly charred. Remove from grill and set aside.
6. Toss the red onion slices in the remaining 1 tablespoon of oil and grill over high heat until caramelized on both sides. Remove from grill and set aside.
7. Grill the potatoes whole over medium heat until browned on all sides and cooked through (200°F), approximately 10 to 15 minutes (depending on their size). Remove from grill and set aside.
8. Peel the loosened skins from the bell peppers and discard the removed skins
9. Cut the peppers, green onions, and red onions into small pieces.
10. Cut the smallest potatoes in half, and the larger ones into quarters to make consistent bite-sized pieces.
11. Gently toss all the cut salad ingredients (potatoes, peppers, green onions, red onions, eggs) with the dressing and serve immediately. If serving it later, it is important to chill the salad ingredients first before mixing with the dressing to ensure the complete salad stays chilled and keep it out of the bacteria danger zone. Remember to always follow the rule: keep cold foods cold and keep hot foods hot.

Makes approximately 8 side dish portions

*Sambal oelek is an Indonesian chili sauce or paste typically made from a mixture of a variety of chili peppers. One can usually find it down the imported (or Asian) food aisle of major grocery stores.

 One large egg has 6.5 grams of protein!

Hot & Sour Soup

"Another Chinese take-out favourite. Black pepper can be substituted for the white pepper, but white pepper is a classic ingredient. Reduce the amount of sambal oelek if you want it milder."

2 tablespoons sesame oil, divided
200g shitake mushrooms, stems discarded, thinly sliced
100g cremini mushrooms, thinly sliced
1/2 teaspoon ground white pepper
2 - 900ml tetra-packs of vegetable broth
227ml can bamboo shoots*, drained
5 tablespoons white vinegar
2 tablespoons grated fresh ginger
1 tablespoon sambal oelek*
1/4 cup cornstarch
1/4 cup soy sauce
2 large eggs, beaten
200g firm tofu, diced 1/2 inch
1 teaspoon white sugar
1/2 teaspoon salt
1 bunch green onions, thinly sliced for garnish

1. Heat a soup pot over medium-high heat. Add 1 tablespoon of the sesame oil, the mushrooms, and the white pepper. Stir to combine and cook, stirring occasionally, for 2 to 3 minutes until the mushrooms are soft and reduced in size.
2. Stir in the vegetable broth, bamboo shoots, vinegar, ginger, and sambal oelek. Bring to a simmer.
3. Dissolve the cornstarch in the soy sauce, and then stir into the soup. Increase the heat to high to bring to a boil.
4. Reduce the heat to low to maintain a slight simmer. Slowly drizzle in the beaten eggs while stirring to create small ribbons of cooked egg throughout the soup.
5. Stir in the tofu, the remaining 1 tablespoon of sesame oil, sugar, and salt. Serve garnished with the green onions.

Makes approximately 10 cups total

*Cans of bamboo shoots can usually be found either down the imported (or Asian) food aisle, or with the canned vegetables near the canned water chestnuts and canned baby corn.

*Sambal oelek is an Indonesian chili sauce or paste typically made from a mixture of a variety of chili peppers. One can usually find it down the imported (or Asian) food aisle of major grocery stores.

PASTA

Fresh Pasta from Scratch – Makes about 1-pound fresh pasta

10oz (approx. 2 cups sifted) 00 Flour or all-purpose flour
2 large eggs
4 large egg yolks
1 teaspoon salt
Extra flour for dusting

1. Mound the flour on a countertop and make a well in the center large enough for the rest of the ingredients.
2. Add the eggs, egg yolks, and salt to the well. Scramble the eggs with a fork and slowly start incorporating the flour. Keep mixing with a fork while continuing to incorporate more flour until you cannot mix with a fork any longer. Continue to mix by hand for a couple of minutes until it comes together in one mass. You may need to add a bit of water if it is too dry or a bit more flour if it is too wet. It should be firm and holding together but not sticky.
3. Knead by hand for approximately 10 minutes until smooth. Shape into a ball, cover with plastic wrap and let sit at room temperature for at least 1 hour. Or alternatively up to 3 hours in the refrigerator.
4. Cut dough into 4 equal pieces and work with one piece at a time while keeping the others covered. Set your pasta machine to the widest setting. Hand shape the piece of dough into an approximate rectangle and feed it through the machine. Fold it over and pass it through again. Dust it with a bit of flour now and run it through the 2nd setting twice.
5. Continue to run it through the machine once each on the remaining settings of the rollers until desired thickness is reached.
6. Stop when the pasta has reached the desired thickness, dust liberally with flour and cut into the desired shape(s). Dust one more time with flour and set aside covered with plastic wrap until all the pasta dough is rolled and cut.
7. Bring salted water to a boil and then add the fresh pasta, stirring immediately and cook until done – anywhere from 1 to 5 minutes depending on the thickness you have chosen. Toss with your favorite sauce and enjoy!

Greek Pastitsio
"A Greek baked pasta dish at its finest"

1 pound (454g) lean ground beef
1 large onion, diced small, approximately 2 cups
4 to 6 garlic cloves, minced
1 tablespoon dried oregano
2 to 3 teaspoons salt
1 teaspoon pepper
1 – 156ml can tomato paste
1 – 796ml can of diced tomatoes
1.5 cups full bodied red wine
2 bay leaves
5 tablespoons butter
6 tablespoons flour
3 cups milk
1 teaspoon salt
1/4 teaspoon pepper
1/4 teaspoon ground nutmeg
2 cups crumbled feta cheese
500g macaroni type pasta
3 large eggs

1. Preheat the oven to 350°F and prepare a 9 x 13 x 2.5 inch baking pan with baking spray.
2. Brown the beef in a large pan over medium heat. Stir in the onion, garlic, oregano, 2 teaspoons of the salt, and the 1 teaspoon pepper. Cook until the onion and garlic are soft, approximately 2 to 3 minutes.
3. Stir in the tomato paste, tomatoes, wine, and bay leaves. Bring to a boil and then simmer until sauce consistency is reached, approximately 10 minutes. Season with the other teaspoon of salt if desired and set aside.
4. In a separate pot melt the butter over low heat. Stir in the flour and cook for approximately 5 minutes, stirring occasionally (this removes the starchy taste of the flour). Add the milk gradually, while whisking constantly, until all the milk has been thoroughly incorporated. Stir in the 1 teaspoon salt, 1/4 teaspoon pepper, and nutmeg. Bring to boil

over medium heat, while stirring occasionally, to thicken this white sauce. Remove from the heat, stir in 1 cup of the crumbled feta cheese, and set aside.

5. Cook your pasta to desired consistency.

6. In a mixing bowl beat the eggs. Gradually add a small amount (approximately 1/3) of your reserved white sauce into the eggs while whisking constantly – this will temper the eggs to come up in temperature gradually without curdling them. Then mix this tempered egg/sauce mixture back into the remaining white sauce.

7. Assemble your pan as follows: one layer of half of the pasta, top with the remaining cup of crumbled feta cheese, top with the meat sauce, top with the remaining pasta, and finally top with the white sauce.

8. Bake in the oven for approximately 30 minutes to set the eggs in the white sauce. Then broil until lightly browned. Let rest for 10 to 15 minutes before cutting as desired and serve.

Makes 9 large portions or 12 smaller portions

German Spaetzle with Sage Browned Butter

3 large eggs
1.5 cups all-purpose flour
1 teaspoon salt
1/4 teaspoon ground nutmeg
6 to 10 tablespoons milk (approximately - see step 1)
2 tablespoons melted butter
1/3 cup cold butter, cubed into 6 equal pieces and kept cold
3 tablespoons chopped fresh sage
1/3 cup finely grated parmesan
Fresh cracked pepper
Salt to taste, if desired
Finely chopped parsley for garnish, optional

1. Bring a large pot of water to a rolling boil.
2. In a medium mixing bowl, beat the eggs. Add the flour, salt, nutmeg, and 6 tablespoons of the milk. Whisk to combine to form a thick batter - you want it to look gluey (thick enough to just slowly run from the whisk). Depending on the exact size of your eggs & how compact or loose the flour measurement is, you may need to add more milk.
3. Using a flat standard hole cheese grater (or spaetzle maker or colander) push 1/3 of the batter through the holes into the pot of boiling water. Cook briefly, while stirring, until they all float, and are cooked, approximately 1 minute. Use a large slotted spoon to remove the cooked spaetzle (and let drain off) and transfer to a bowl and toss with the 2 tablespoons of melted butter. Repeat 2 more times until all the spaetzle batter has been cooked and set aside in that bowl.
4. Heat a cast iron pan over medium-high heat. Once hot add the 6 cubes of cold butter. As soon as the butter has half melted add the sage and stir constantly until the butter foam looks slightly golden, and then remove from the pan and stir into the reserved spaetzle immediately.
5. Toss the spaetzle with the parmesan, a few grinds of fresh cracked pepper, and season to taste with salt. Serve garnished with parsley.

Makes approximately 3.5 cups total

Pasta Carbonara

"This recipe is for one portion - times by 2 for 2 people; times by 4 for 4 people, etc. This is my version of this classic pasta dish - Traditional Italian carbonara uses guanciale (cured pig cheek) or pancetta, no cream, and no peas."

100g long dry pasta (spaghetti, linguine, fettucine, etc.)
1 to 2 strips thick bacon, cut into 1/4-inch pieces
1/3 cup frozen peas
1 large egg
1/3 cup finely grated Parmesan cheese
2 to 3 tablespoons 18%MF cream
Salt & pepper to taste

1. Bring a pot of salted water to a boil and cook your pasta until desired doneness.
2. Fry bacon in a non-stick pan over medium to medium-high heat until mostly crisp, stirring occasionally. Turn off the burner but keep the bacon in the pan on the stove.
3. Don't drain the pasta in a colander - instead, using tongs, grab the pasta from the water and transfer to the pan with the bacon, letting some of the water go into the pan with the pasta.
4. Add the peas to the pan. Whisk the egg, cheese, and cream together and pour over the pasta. Immediately, with the tongs, toss the pasta in the pan until the sauce becomes thicker and coats the pasta. It is important to make sure this environment is not too hot as that would curdle the egg. We want the egg to cook slowly in the residual heat of the hot pasta, bacon, and the pan.
5. Season to taste with salt & pepper and serve immediately as you cannot reheat this sauce without overcooking the eggs.

Makes 1 portion

Mushroom Spaetzle with Poached Eggs

Recipe Courtesy of BC Egg, bcegg.com

1/4 cup butter
2 tablespoons canola oil
1.5 cups sliced mushrooms (mixed varieties)
2 teaspoons salt, divided
3 garlic cloves, minced
7 large eggs, divided
1.5 cups all-purpose flour
1/8 teaspoon ground nutmeg
6 to 8 tablespoons milk (approximately - see step 3)
2 tablespoons white vinegar
3 tablespoons chopped fresh parsley
Salt and fresh cracked pepper to taste
2 tablespoons chopped fresh chives, for garnish

1. Heat a large skillet over medium heat. Add the butter and canola oil and heat until the butter has melted and starts to foam. Add the mushrooms and 1 teaspoon of the salt. Stir to combine and cook for approximately 3 to 4 minutes, stirring occasionally, until the mushrooms are soft and browned slightly.
2. Turn heat to low, stir in the garlic, and cook for an additional 2 to 3 minutes. Turn off the heat and let stand on the stovetop while making the spaetzle.
3. In a medium mixing bowl, beat 3 of the eggs. Add the flour, the other 1 teaspoon salt, nutmeg, and 6 tablespoons of the milk. Whisk to combine to form a thick batter - you want it to look gluey (thick enough to just slowly run from the whisk). Depending on the exact size of your eggs and how compact or loose the flour measurement is, you may need to add more (or use less) milk.
4. Bring a large pot of water to a rolling boil.
5. Using a flat standard hole cheese grater (or spaetzle maker or colander) push 1/3 of the batter through the holes into the pot of boiling water. Cook briefly, while stirring, until they all float, approximately 1 minute. Use a large, slotted spoon to remove the cooked spaetzle (and let drain

off) and transfer to the cooked mushroom mixture. Repeat this 2 more times until all the spaetzle batter has been cooked and added to the mushroom mixture.

6. In a large pan of simmering water, add the vinegar. Poach the 4 remaining eggs until the whites are no longer translucent and the yolks are soft, approximately 3 minutes.

7. While the eggs are poaching, turn the heat for the mushroom/spaetzle mixture to medium-high and add the chopped parsley. Stir to combine and sauté briefly to warm up. Season to taste with salt and pepper and then portion this mixture equally into 4 serving bowls.

8. Remove the cooked poached eggs one at a time with a slotted spoon, dabbing on paper towel, and transfer each egg to top each of the each of the 4 portioned spaetzle dishes. Garnish with the chopped chives and a sprinkle of salt and pepper on the egg (if desired) and serve immediately.

Makes 4 portions

Potato Gnocchi from Scratch

"No matter how you pronounce it, Gnocchi is a potato based Italian pasta that is shaped like little dumplings and tastes amazing. The ridges and indentations of the finished shapes help to hold sauce."

1-pound (454g) russet potatoes, peeled
1.5 packed cups all-purpose flour*
2.25 teaspoons baking powder
1.5 teaspoons salt
1 large egg
Extra flour for dusting/shaping

1. Diced the peeled potatoes into approximately 1/2-inch cubes. Steam for 20 to 25 minutes until tender.
2. For best results place the cooked potatoes through a ricer into a mixing bowl for a fine texture. Alternatively, you can thoroughly mash the cooked potatoes, or push the potatoes through a wire strainer, but ricing is better. Let cool slightly before proceeding to the next step.
3. Add the flour, baking powder, salt, and egg to the potatoes. Stir until the dough just starts coming together. Then knead for approximately 2 minutes until a smooth (not sticky) dough is formed. If the dough is sticky, add a bit more flour. If the dough is too dry, wet your hands with a bit of water. Unlike regular homemade pasta, don't knead your gnocchi dough too long otherwise they will become tough.
4. Divide the dough into 8 equal pieces. Working with 1 piece at a time, shape and roll it into a 1/2-inch diameter long rope shape. Cut the shape into 1/2-inch pieces and gently toss in extra flour to keep from sticking to each other. With 2 fingers push each gnocchi piece against a gnocchi paddle (or the tines of a fork works well, or the texture of a cheese grater) to create indents and ridges.
5. Bring salted water to a boil. Boil 1/4 or 1/2 of the gnocchi recipe at a time, boiling for approximately 3 minutes. Use a large slotted spoon to transfer the cooked gnocchi to a strainer. Then add more gnocchi to the boiling water. Add drained gnocchi to desired sauce to coat. Serve immediately.

Makes approximately 1.5 pounds of fresh gnocchi

*NOTE: If the potatoes are fresh, then the flour needs to be packed. If the potatoes are older (and thus drier) you won't need as much flour.

 Did you know that 100% of egg farms in BC are family owned and operated?

BEEF, LAMB, & POULTRY

Greek Lamb (or Beef) Burgers

"Ideally served with freshly made tzatziki along with lettuce on your favourite burger buns. I also like to add a slice of tomato, but that's optional."

500g lean ground lamb (or lean ground beef, if preferred)
1 large egg
7 garlic cloves, finely minced
3 tablespoons finely chopped fresh oregano
2 tablespoons finely chopped fresh rosemary
1 teaspoon salt
1/2 teaspoon pepper
100g feta cheese, crumbled
Lettuce
4 thick tomato slices, optional
4 hamburger buns of your choice

1. Mix all ingredients in a bowl and divide equally into four portions. Shape each portion into a burger patty.
2. On a preheated BBQ, grill the burgers over medium flame until cooked through or alternatively in a preheated pan over medium heat. Approximately 4 to 5 minutes per side but an instant read thermometer is the way to go: 71°C or 160°F.
3. Serve with Tzatziki, and lettuce, and optional tomato on your favourite burger buns.

Makes 4 burgers

 Eggs travel from the farm to your grocery store shelves in just 4 to 10 days in BC - now that's farm fresh!

Almond Chicken

"A classic Chinese Take-Out favourite! An oil thermometer is a must for this recipe. If you can't find almond flour, then substitute with all-purpose flour."

Canola oil for frying
2 boneless skinless chicken breasts, approximately 1-pound (454g) total
6 tablespoons almond flour, divided
1/2 teaspoon salt
1/4 teaspoon pepper
2 tablespoons all-purpose flour
4 tablespoons cornstarch
1/2 teaspoon baking powder
2 large eggs, beaten
Fine Kosher salt or sea salt
Shredded iceberg lettuce, for plating
1/4 cup chopped blanched almonds, toasted

1. In a large deep pot, add enough canola oil for about a 3-inch to 4-inch depth of oil. Heat the oil until you can maintain a consistent temperature of 370°F to 380°F.
2. Butterfly cut the thicker part of the chicken breasts to make them more uniform in thickness. Place each chicken breast between two pieces of wax paper or plastic wrap. Using the flat side of a meat tenderizer mallet, flatten the chicken breasts to a uniform thickness of approximately 1/2 inch.
3. On a dinner plate, combine 4 tablespoons of the almond flour with the 1/2 teaspoon salt and 1/4 teaspoon of pepper and set aside.
4. In a large mixing bowl, combine the remaining 2 tablespoons of almond flour with the all-purpose flour, cornstarch, and baking powder. Then whisk in the beaten eggs to make a batter – it should be the consistency of pancake batter.
5. Work with 1 chicken breast at a time as follows: dredge the flattened chicken breast in the seasoned almond flour mixture until lightly coated. Then coat with a thin layer of batter and carefully and slowly add to the hot oil. Fry until golden brown and crispy, approximately 5 minutes total, and turn the chicken over in the oil at the halfway mark.

The internal temperature should be at least 160 degrees Fahrenheit. Once done, transfer to a wire rack and immediately dust with the Kosher salt and sprinkle with some toasted almonds.

6. Once both chicken breasts are done, prepare a serving dish with a layer of shredded iceberg lettuce.
7. Slice the chicken into 1/2-inch strips and place on the lettuce. Sprinkle with any remaining almonds and serve immediately.

Makes approximately 4 portions

Italian Meatballs

"The perfect addition to your pasta sauce to make spaghetti & meatballs"

250g ground chuck (or ground beef)
250g ground pork
1 large egg
1/4 cup fine breadcrumbs
1/4 cup finely grated parmesan cheese
2 tablespoons minced onion
1 tablespoon finely crushed or minced garlic
1 tablespoon dried basil
2 teaspoons red wine vinegar
1 teaspoon salt
1/2 teaspoon pepper

1. Preheat oven to 400°F. Line a baking sheet with parchment paper or spray with baking spray and set aside.
2. In a large bowl, combine all the ingredients together thoroughly. Roll bits of the mixture into small meatballs approximately 3/4 inch in size and place them on the prepared baking sheet. You should have approximately 25 to 30 meatballs.
3. Bake in the preheated oven for approximately 20 minutes, or until their internal temperature reaches 160°F (71°C). Add to your favorite tomato pasta sauce and enjoy!

Makes 25 to 30 meatballs

Crispy Pan-Fried Chicken Fingers

"Actually, shallow frying (less oil than pan frying or deep frying), but still crispy and delicious. Breast filets are the strips that come off the underside of chicken breasts and are usually available to purchase separately from the chicken breasts."

1/2 cup all-purpose flour
1.5 teaspoons salt
1 teaspoon baking powder
1 teaspoon garlic powder
1 teaspoon onion powder
3/4 teaspoon paprika or smoked paprika
1/2 teaspoon pepper
2 large eggs
2 tablespoons cold water
1.5 cups Corn Flake crumbs
16 chicken breast filets
1/2 cup canola oil
Extra salt for dusting
Serve with Honey Mustard Sauce (in the "Spreads, Dips & Salsas chapter)

1. On a large plate, toss together the following ingredients and set aside: flour, salt, baking powder, garlic powder, onion powder, paprika, and pepper.
2. In a medium mixing bowl, beat together the eggs and water and set aside.
3. Place the Corn Flake crumbs on another large plate and set aside.
4. Dredge all the chicken breast filets in the seasoned flour.
5. Then, working with 2 or 3 at a time, dip the filets into the egg mixture (called an 'egg wash') while draining each one a bit by running it up the side of the bowl before transferring to the crumbs (called the 'breading'). Coat liberally until completely coated with Corn Flake crumbs and then set aside on a tray. Repeat with all the filets.
6. Heat a 10" skillet (I prefer cast iron because it holds heat so well) over medium heat. Add the oil and heat the oil for about 3 to 4 minutes until hot. You can test the oil by partially dipping in one of the coated filets (you should hear it sizzling).

7. Working with 4 filets in the pan a t a time (4 batches total for the complete recipe 4 x 4 = 16 filets), pan fry on the first side for 4 minutes until golden brown and crispy. Flip them over and pan-fry for another 3 to 4 minutes until the second side is golden brown and the filets are cooked completely through. Internal temperature should be minimum 71 degrees Celsius or 165 degrees Fahrenheit.
8. Transfer the cooked filets to drain on paper towel, and immediately dust with the optional salt if desired. Let cool a bit before serving.

Makes 16 chicken fingers

Chicken Fried Rice

"Another classic Chinese Take-Out favourite. If you have it, a higher heat oil, like extra virgin avocado oil, is even better than canola oil."

4 teaspoons canola oil, separated
2 large eggs, beaten
3/4-pound (340g) chicken breast or thigh, boneless skinless, cut small pieces
Salt & pepper
1/2 cup small diced onion
1 small carrot, diced small, approximately 1/3 cup
1 tablespoon finely minced or grated ginger
1 cup frozen peas
4 cups cold pre-cooked rice
3 garlic cloves, finely minced or crushed in garlic press
1 teaspoon chicken stock paste*
1 tablespoon oyster sauce*
2 tablespoons soy sauce*
1/2 teaspoon ground turmeric
1 tablespoon butter
1 tablespoon sesame oil*
4 green onions, sliced 1/4 inch

1. Heat a large pan or wok over medium-high heat. Add 2 teaspoons of the canola oil and then the beaten eggs. Cook for about 30 seconds while breaking up until completely cooked into small bits.
2. Add the chicken to the egg and season lightly with some salt & pepper. Cook while stirring frequently for about 2 minutes until chicken is mostly cooked.
3. Add the other 2 teaspoons canola oil, then the onion, carrot, and ginger. Cook, stirring frequently, until onion and carrot are mostly soft, approximately 2 minutes.
4. Stir in the frozen peas. Thoroughly stir in the rice and garlic and cook for about 1 minute, making sure to break up any lumps of rice.
5. In a small bowl, whisk the chicken stock paste together with the oyster sauce. Then whisk in the soy sauce to this mixture. Stir this mixture

thoroughly into the rice with the turmeric and cook for about 1 more minute until the rice is completely heated, stirring frequently.

6. Stir in the butter, sesame oil, and green onions. Continue stirring until the butter has completely melted. Season to taste with more soy sauce (or salt & pepper) if desired and serve immediately.

Makes approximately 6 cups

NOTES

*Chicken stock paste is chicken broth that has been reduced down to a concentrated paste form. The most common brand found at your local grocery stores is "Better Than Bouillon" Chicken Base – in small glass jars. Once opened this will last 1 year easily in your refrigerator.

*Oyster sauce, soy sauce and sesame oil can all be found down the Asian/Import food aisle of your major grocery store.

Guinness Shepherd's Pie

"A classic Irish pub favourite! Shepherd's Pie made with ground beef instead of the traditional ground lamb is actually called a Cottage Pie, but I kept the name Shepherd's Pie because it is more recognizable."

4 large russet potatoes, peeled and diced 1/2-inch
2 pounds (908g) lean ground beef
1 cup small-diced onion
1 cup small-diced carrot
1 cup small-diced celery
6 garlic cloves, minced
1/4 cup flour
1 tablespoon dried oregano
1 tablespoon dried thyme
4 teaspoons salt, divided
1.5 teaspoons ground black pepper, divided
1.5 teaspoons beef stock paste
1 – 156ml can tomato paste
1 – 440ml can Guinness beer
2 tablespoons sugar
1 tablespoon Worcestershire sauce
1 cup frozen peas
1/2 cup butter, cubed
1 large egg
1/4 cup whipping cream

1. Preheat the oven to 400°F.
2. Steam the potatoes for 20 minutes or until tender, set aside but keep warm over the water.
3. While the potatoes are steaming, brown the beef in a large pan over medium heat until all the liquid from the beef has evaporated, approximately 15 to 20 minutes.
4. To the beef, add the onion, carrot, celery, garlic, flour, oregano, thyme, 2 teaspoons of the salt, and 1 teaspoon of the pepper. Cook until softened a bit, approximately 5 to 7 minutes.
5. Stir in the beef stock paste and tomato paste until evenly distributed.

6. Stir in the Guinness, sugar, Worcestershire, and peas. Taste and re-season with salt and pepper if necessary. Remove from heat and let stand while mashing the potatoes.
7. Add the butter, remaining 2 teaspoons salt, and remaining 1/2 teaspoon pepper to the steamed potatoes and mash together until smooth.
8. In a small bowl thoroughly beat the egg and whipping cream together. Slowly add this to the mashed potatoes while incorporating to ensure that the egg doesn't become scrambled. Taste and re-season with salt and pepper if necessary.
9. Put the beef mixture into a 9 x 13 inch cake pan or casserole dish. Top evenly with the mashed potatoes and run a fork over the potatoes to make a design.
10. Bake for 30 minutes until the potato starts to brown. Let sit for at least 10 minutes before serving.

Makes approximately 8 to 12 portions

Honey Garlic Meatballs

"Combining two different types of meat gives the meatballs more complex flavour and seasoned with Chinese 5 Spice powder they are perfect with this sauce. Ground chuck is beef but has more flavour than ground beef from the supermarket – visit your local butcher to get some."

Meatballs
1 pound (454g) ground chuck (or ground beef)
1 pound (454g) lean ground pork
2 large eggs
1/2 cup fine breadcrumbs
1/4 cup minced onion
2 tablespoons finely crushed or minced garlic
1 tablespoon Chinese 5 Spice powder
2 teaspoons salt
1 teaspoon ground black pepper

Sauce
1 cup + 2 tablespoons beef broth
3/4 cup dark brown sugar
1/2 cup liquid honey
6 tablespoons soy sauce
3 tablespoons cornstarch
1.5 tablespoons finely crushed garlic
1/2 teaspoon salt

1. Preheat oven to 400°F. Spray a baking sheet with baking spray and set aside.
2. In a large bowl, combine the chuck, pork, eggs, breadcrumbs, onion, garlic, 5 spice, 2 teaspoons salt & the pepper. Mix until thoroughly combined into a homogenous mixture. Roll bits of the mixture into small meatballs approximately 3/4-inch in size and place them on the prepared baking sheet. You should have approximately 45 to 50 meatballs. Bake in the preheated oven for approximately 15 to 20 minutes, or until their internal temperature reaches 160°F (71°C).

3. While the meatballs are cooking, prepare the sauce by combining the beef broth, brown sugar, honey, soy sauce, cornstarch, garlic and 1/2 teaspoon salt in a medium heavy-bottomed pot. Place on medium-high heat and bring to a boil stirring occasionally. When it just starts to boil stir constantly until it has reached a full rolling boil. It must reach a full boil to activate the cornstarch thickener fully. Remove from the heat and set aside.

4. Place the cooked meatballs on paper towel temporarily to remove some of the fat. Transfer the meatballs to a serving dish, cover with the sauce and serve immediately with or without cooked rice.

Makes 45 to 50, 3/4-inch meatballs

Sweet & Sour Meatballs

Use the same recipe & instructions from the Honey Garlic Meatballs, except substitute 1 tablespoon chilli powder for the 1 tablespoon Chinese 5 spice powder, and use these sauce ingredients instead for the sauce:

Sauce
2 cups white sugar
1 & 1/2 cups white vinegar
1/2 cup brown sugar
1/2 cup ketchup
1/2 cup soy sauce
4 & 1/2 tablespoons cornstarch

Moist Classic Meatloaf

"The moistest meatloaf you will ever have. A family classic reinvented!"

Meatloaf

3 pounds (1.36kg) lean ground beef
3 large eggs
2 onions, finely chopped
2 cloves of garlic, minced
2 cups breadcrumbs
1.5 cups milk
6 tablespoons ketchup
2 tablespoons Worcestershire sauce
3 teaspoons salt
2 teaspoons ground black pepper

Sauce

1 cup ketchup
1/2 cup white sugar
1/4 cup red wine vinegar

1. Preheat oven to 350°F.
2. Prepare 2 standard loaf pans with baking spray, butter, or line with parchment paper.
3. In a large bowl, mix together the meat loaf ingredients: ground beef, eggs, onions, garlic, breadcrumbs, milk, 6 tablespoons ketchup, Worcestershire, salt, and pepper.
4. Divide this mixture equally between the 2 prepared pans and press down to make an even flat surface on the meat loaves.
5. Mix the 3 sauce ingredients together and distribute evenly over the 2 meat loaves.
6. Bake in the preheated oven until the internal temperature reaches 71°C, or 165°F, approximately 1 hour.
7. Let cool in pans for at least 20 minutes before slicing and serving.

Makes 2 meat loaves

Saucy Little Meat Loaves

"My Aunt Shirley used to make something like this for me when I was a kid – one of my favourite meals of hers! Individual meat loaves with a zesty sauce – loaded with flavour."

1.5 pounds (680g) lean ground beef
1 large egg
1/2 cup quick oats
1/4 cup minced onion
4 cloves garlic, minced or crushed to a paste
1 tablespoon dark brown sugar
1.5 teaspoons salt
1 teaspoon chili powder
1 teaspoon dried basil leaves
1/2 teaspoon pepper
1 – 680ml can of tomato sauce
1/2 cup blueberry jam or grape jelly
1/4 cup dark brown sugar
4 teaspoons cornstarch
2 teaspoons Worcestershire sauce
1 teaspoon salt
1/4 teaspoon pepper

1. Preheat oven to 400°F.
2. Combine the ground beef with the egg, oats, onion, garlic, 1 tablespoon brown sugar, 1.5 teaspoons salt, chili powder, basil, 1/2 teaspoon pepper, and 1/2 cup of the tomato sauce. Shape into 6 ovals (loaves) in a shallow baking dish and bake for 20 minutes.
3. Combine the remaining tomato sauce, jam/jelly, 1/4 cup brown sugar, cornstarch, Worcestershire, 1 teaspoon salt and 1/4 teaspoon pepper in a bowl.
4. At the end of the 20 minute baking time, remove the fat from the pan and pour the sauce mixture over the loaves. Bake 10 minutes longer.

Makes 6 portions

PORK

Bacon & Egg Breakfast Casserole

Recipe Courtesy of BC Egg, bcegg.com

4 – 6 slices of sandwich bread, cut into quarters
4 thick slices of bacon, diced
3/4 cup shredded aged cheddar cheese, divided
1 cup sliced mushrooms
6 large eggs
1.5 cups milk
3/4 teaspoon salt
1 cup frozen hash brown potatoes, thawed
1/2 teaspoon ground black pepper

1. Spray 9-inch square baking pan with cooking spray (a 7x11" pan works well too). Arrange bread slices in pan, overlapping slightly.
2. Cook bacon in a pan over medium to medium-high heat until crisp. Remove the cooked bacon with a slotted spoon and sprinkle evenly over the bread in the pan, along with 1/4 cup of the cheese.
3. Add the mushrooms to the pan with the bacon fat and cook until browned. Remove the cooked mushrooms with a slotted spoon and sprinkle evenly over the bread, bacon, and cheese.
4. Whisk the eggs thoroughly with the milk and salt. Pour this mixture over the bread slices and toppings.
5. Add the thawed hash browns to the pan with the bacon fat, increase the heat to medium-high, and cook until just starting to brown. Remove with a slotted spoon and sprinkle evenly over the prepared dish along with the remaining 1/2 cup cheese.
6. Sprinkle the pepper over the dish and wrap with plastic wrap. Refrigerate for a few hours or overnight.
7. Preheat oven to 350°F. Remove and discard the plastic wrap and bake until browned on top and an inserted knife in the centre comes out clean, approximately 35 minutes. Let rest 5 minutes before cutting into 6 portions and serving.

Makes 6 portions

Bacon Gruyere Quiche

Recipe Courtesy of BC Egg, bcegg.com

"This recipe was developed by young farmer Kaelen, of Brightside eggs. She recommends blending the sautéed onions with the cream, to give the quiche extra creaminess!"

1 unbaked pie shell
300g bacon, chopped
1 medium onion, chopped
2 cloves garlic, minced
1 cup whipping heavy cream
6 large eggs
8 oz (226 g) Gruyere cheese, grated
2 oz (56 g) cheddar cheese, grated
1/2 teaspoon salt
1/4 teaspoon ground black pepper
Chopped chives or green onions

1. Preheat oven 350°F. Put unbaked pie shell in standard 9-inch pie plate.
2. In a medium non-stick frying pan over medium to medium-high heat, cook the bacon until crisp, stirring occasionally. Remove with a slotted spoon and set aside. Keep 2 tablespoons of the bacon fat in the pan and discard the rest of the bacon fat.
3. To the 2 tablespoons of bacon fat in the pan over medium heat, add the onion and garlic. Cook, stirring occasionally, until the onions are soft, approximately 2 to 3 minutes.
4. This step is optional but will help achieve a creamier quiche. Using an immersion blender or in a regular blender, blend the sautéed onions and garlic with the cream until it is well incorporated and there are no large chunks remaining, approximately 30 seconds.
5. Beat the eggs together in a large mixing bowl. Add the onion-cream mixture, the reserved cooked bacon, both cheeses, salt, and pepper. Mix thoroughly.
6. Pour the egg mixture into the pie shell. Sprinkle with chopped chives or green onions.

7. Bake for 40-45 minutes, or until the edges are golden brown and the centre is set. Let it rest for 10 minutes before cutting into 6 or 8 pieces. Serve it warm or chill it and serve it cold with a salad or fresh fruit.

Makes 6 to 8 portions

Breakfast Fold Over

Recipe Courtesy of BC Egg, bcegg.com

"Feel free to customize these however you want with different kinds of cheese, swap the ham for bacon or cooked and crumbled sausage, try some veggies, and more."

1 tablespoon butter
2 large eggs
Salt & pepper
1 ten-inch flour tortilla
Sliced deli ham
1/4 cup grated cheddar cheese
1 tablespoon minced green onion

1. In a medium sized non-stick pan, melt the butter over medium low heat. Crack the eggs into a small bowl, whisk them with a bit of salt & pepper, and then pour the eggs into the pan. Stir the eggs with a spatula while they cook. You want to move the eggs around while curds form and the raw egg flows underneath. When the eggs are cooked, remove them from the pan to a plate and wipe the pan clean with paper towel.
2. Lay the tortilla on the counter in front of you. Top one half of it with sliced ham, then eggs, cheese, and a bit of minced green onion.
3. Fold the other half of the tortilla over the filling. Place the folded tortilla in the pan over medium heat. Cook until golden and then flip over to cook the other side.
4. Remove the fold over to a plate and cut into triangles. Serve with salsa or ketchup for dipping!

Makes 1 portion

Butternut Squash & Shallot Hash – makes 4 portions
Recipe Courtesy of BC Egg, bcegg.com

4 teaspoons olive oil
1/2 cup chopped shallots
1/3 cup diced pancetta
1 red bell pepper, chopped
1 tablespoon finely chopped fresh rosemary
Pinch hot pepper flakes
2.5 oz (70g) cubed butternut squash
1/4 teaspoon salt
1/4 teaspoon pepper
1/2 cup low-sodium chicken broth
3 tablespoons butter, divided
1 tablespoon apple cider vinegar
1 tablespoon honey
4 large eggs
Salt & pepper
1/4 cup grated parmesan cheese
2 tablespoons finely chopped fresh chives

1. Heat 2 teaspoons of the oil in large skillet set over medium heat; cook shallots, pancetta, red pepper, rosemary, and hot pepper flakes for 3 to 5 minutes or until vegetables start to soften and pancetta starts to brown. Remove from pan.
2. Add the remaining 2 teaspoons oil to the pan if needed, and add butternut squash, salt, and pepper. Cook, stirring occasionally, for 5 to 7 minutes or until squash starts to brown. Stir in broth, 1 tablespoon of the butter, vinegar and honey.
3. Cover and cook for 6 to 8 minutes or until liquid is absorbed and squash is tender. (Note: cook time may vary depending on the size of your squash cubes.) Add the reserved pancetta and pepper mixture back to the skillet and mix through.
4. Meanwhile, melt remaining 2 tablespoons butter in non-stick skillet set over medium heat; break eggs into skillet. Season with salt and pepper.

Cover and cook for 2 to 3 minutes or until eggs whites are just set for sunny-side up or cook until done as desired.

5. Sprinkle hash with Parmesan and chives and divide among 4 plates. Top each serving with fried egg and enjoy!

Egg Stuffed Bell Peppers – makes 4 portions
Recipe Courtesy of BC Egg, bcegg.com

4 large bell peppers (red, yellow, or orange)
Olive oil
Salt and pepper
Garlic powder
1 cup diced tomato
1 cup sliced mushrooms
1 cup chopped cooked bacon, divided
1 cup grated mozzarella cheese
4 large eggs
1 cup grated cheddar cheese
2 green onions, thinly sliced

1. Preheat oven to 375°F and line a baking sheet with parchment paper.
2. Lay the bell peppers on their sides. Leaving stems intact, cut the 1/4 of the bell peppers off and core/discard the seeds and white membrane. Take the parts of the bell pepper that were cut off and diced them small and set aside.
3. Brush the insides of the bell pepper with olive oil and sprinkle with salt, pepper, and garlic powder. Fill the bell peppers equally with the diced tomato, mushrooms, 1/2 cup of the cooked bacon, the reserved diced bell pepper from step 2, and the mozzarella cheese.
4. Crack 1 egg into each of the 4 bell peppers and season with more salt and pepper. Top equally with the cheddar cheese, remaining 1/2 cup cooked bacon, and the green onions.
5. Placed the filled bell peppers on the prepared baking sheet and bakes for approximately 15 to 20 minutes or until the egg whites are just set and the egg yolks are still runny.

Egg & Chorizo Taco Filling

"A great way to incorporate nutritious eggs into Taco Night! Use this filling for any Mexican meal applications, such as tacos, burritos, quesadillas, etc. Everything you need in one pan – just scoop, fill, and serve!"

1 tablespoon canola oil
1 recipe of raw chorizo sausage meat (recipe below) *
6 large eggs, beaten
175g aged white cheddar, grated, about 1.5 cups
1/2 cup small diced yellow bell pepper
1/2 cup small, diced tomatoes
1/2 cup small diced red onion, rinsed and drained for milder flavour
1 large jalapeno, seeds & membrane removed if desired, diced very small
1 small handful fresh cilantro, chopped
1/2 lime
Taco shells or tortillas, depending on the application
Serve with salsa and sour cream, if desired

1. In a medium non-stick pan on medium-high heat, add the oil and the chorizo. Cook until browned, approximately 10 minutes, while breaking up into small pieces with a wooden spoon.
2. Stir in the BC Eggs and cook while stirring constantly until the eggs are fully cooked and combined with the chorizo, approximately 2 minutes.
3. Turn off the heat and stir in the grated cheese so it can melt.
4. Then evenly top this cooked mixture with the bell pepper, tomatoes, red onion, jalapeno sand cilantro. Squeeze the 1/2 lime over the mixture and serve immediately to fill taco shells or tortillas.

Makes 6 cups of filling, or up to 8 - 12 servings

NOTES
*To make the raw chorizo sausage meat, combine the following ingredients in a bowl:

500g ground pork, 2 tablespoons sweet smoked paprika, 2 tablespoons apple cider vinegar, 1 tablespoon granulated garlic or garlic powder, 2 teaspoons salt, 1 teaspoon dried oregano, 1 teaspoon ground coriander, 1 teaspoon ground cumin, 1/2 – 1 teaspoon ground cayenne, 1/2 teaspoon pepper, 1/4 teaspoon ground cinnamon, 1/4 teaspoon ground cloves

Spicy Chorizo & Tomato Frittata – makes 4 portions
Recipe Courtesy of BC Egg, bcegg.com

8 large eggs
3/4 cup whipping cream
1 teaspoon salt
1/4 teaspoon pepper
1 teaspoon olive oil
2 cloves garlic, thinly sliced
1 small red onion, thinly sliced
1 yellow bell pepper, finely diced
2 chorizo sausages, casings removed, chopped
1 cup cherry tomatoes, cut in half
1/2 cup grated Pepper Jack cheese
2 tablespoons parsley leaves
2 tablespoons cilantro leaves

1. Preheat oven to 375°F.
2. In a large bowl, whisk the eggs, cream, salt, and pepper together. Set aside.
3. Heat the oil in a large ovenproof skillet over medium high heat. Add the garlic, onion, bell pepper, and chorizo. Cook for 4-5 minutes until the onion and peppers are soft and the chorizo is completely cooked through.
4. Reduce heat to medium low. Add the reserved egg mixture and tomatoes to the pan and stir until just combined.
5. Move pan to oven and bake for 10-12 minutes, or until just set. Sprinkle the cheese on top and bake for another 5 minutes until egg has fully set and cheese has melted. Top with parsley and cilantro leaves.

Egg Foo Young - Makes 4 portions, or 8 half-portions
"Another great Chinese take-out favourite"

Egg Foo Young
4 large eggs, beaten
6 tablespoons finely grated carrot
4 tablespoons finely chopped cabbage (green, savoy, napa, etc.)
4 tablespoons thinly sliced green onion
2 teaspoons sambal oelek*
4 teaspoons soy sauce
2 teaspoons oyster sauce
2 teaspoons finely grated fresh ginger
2 teaspoons canola oil
100g ground pork
Finely sliced chives, for garnish
Sesame seeds, for garnish

Sauce
1.5 teaspoons cornstarch
1.5 teaspoons oyster sauce
1.5 teaspoons soy sauce
1/2 teaspoon sugar
1/2 cup low-sodium chicken broth

1. In a 2-cup sized measuring cup (or larger) thoroughly combine the eggs, carrot, cabbage, green onion, sambal oelek, 4 teaspoons soy sauce, 2 teaspoons oyster sauce, and ginger. Set aside.
2. Heat a small 8-inch non-stick pan over medium-high to high heat. Add the oil and the ground pork, and cook, stirring occasionally, until the pork is browned and crispy, about 7 to 8 minutes. Remove from the pan and strain through a wire strainer, reserving the pork and fat separately.
3. Stir in the cooked pork (<u>not</u> the separate reserved fat) into the egg mixture from step #1.
4. In the same small pan, pour a rounded 1/3 cup measure of the egg/pork mixture, and smooth out. Cook over medium-high to high

heat for approximately 2 minutes until the egg mixture has set and the underside has browned. Carefully flip it over and cook the other side for 1 minute until the second side has also browned. Remove from the pan and cover with foil to keep warm.

5. Repeat step #4 three more times, <u>but</u> by <u>first</u> adding a 1/2 teaspoon of the reserved fat to the heated empty pan each time.

6. While cooking the egg mixture, combine the sauce ingredients in a separate small pot and bring to a full boil to thicken. Remove the sauce from the pot and set aside.

7. Garnish the cooked Egg Foo Young with the sauce, chopped chives, and sesame seeds.

*Sambal oelek is an Indonesian chili sauce or paste typically made from a mixture of a variety of chili peppers. One can usually find it down the imported (or Asian) food aisle of major grocery stores.

Individual Monte Cristo Bread Pudding

"The classic Monte Cristo Sandwich but prepared like a bread pudding in an individual baking dish. By preparing this the night before, it makes for a quick gourmet breakfast in the morning."

2 thick slices of sandwich bread
50g ham, diced small
40g Gruyere or Gouda cheese, grated
1 large egg
1/3 cup milk
1 tablespoon finely chopped onion
1/4 teaspoon Worcestershire sauce
1/8 teaspoon dry mustard
1/8 teaspoon salt
Pinch of pepper
1 to 2 drops Tabasco brand sauce
Finely chopped fresh parsley for garnish, optional

1. Cube 1 slice of the bread into approximately 1/2 inch cubes and place them in the bottom of a 2-cup oven-proof dish.
2. Top with the ham, 20g of cheese, and the second slice of bread, cubed.
3. In a small bowl, mix thoroughly together the egg, milk, onion, Worcestershire, mustard, salt, pepper, and Tabasco, and pour over the bread, ham, and cheese in the dish.
4. Top with the second 20g of grated cheese. Cover with plastic wrap and refrigerate overnight for the bread to soak up the egg mixture.
5. Preheat oven to 350°F.
6. Remove the plastic wrap and bake uncovered for approximately 35 to 45 minutes until the egg has cooked through and the cheese has browned. Let stand for 5 minutes, garnish with parsley and serve.

Makes 1 individual portion. *Helpful Tip: If mixing the egg mixture for more than one recipe (one portion) do not add the onion to the egg mixture. Instead add the 1 tbsp chopped onion directly onto the top layer of cubed bread for each portion and pour the egg mixture over top. This will ensure that each portion gets the right amount of onion.

Monte Cristo Breakfast Casserole

"The classic Monte Cristo Sandwich, but prepared in a breakfast casserole format"

12 slices of sandwich bread
300g ham slices
300g Swiss or Emmentaler cheese, grated
1/3 cup finely chopped onion
6 large eggs, beaten
2 cups milk
2 teaspoons Worcestershire sauce
1 teaspoon dry mustard
1 teaspoon salt
8 to 16 drops Tabasco sauce
1/2 teaspoon pepper
Finely chopped fresh parsley for garnish, optional

1. Prepare a 9x13 oven safe dish with baking spray or butter.
2. Arrange 6 slices of the bread in the oven safe dish.
3. Top evenly with the ham, then 200g of the cheese, the chopped onion, and the next 6 slices of bread.
4. In a bowl, mix thoroughly together the eggs, milk, Worcestershire, mustard, salt, and Tabasco. Pour this mixture over the bread, ham, and cheese in the dish, and then sprinkle evenly with the pepper.
5. Top with the remaining 100g of grated cheese. Cover and refrigerate for at least one hour, up to 12 hours, for the bread to soak up the egg mixture.
6. Preheat oven to 350°F.
7. Remove the cover from the dish and bake uncovered for approximately 35 to 40 minutes until the egg has cooked through and the top has browned. Let stand for 5 minutes, garnish with parsley if desired and serve.

Makes 6 portions

Sausage & Egg Breakfast Sandwiches

Recipe Courtesy of Chef Dez & Mrs. Chef Dez, chefdez.com

"Not just for breakfast! These sandwiches are great for any meal. Double the sausage patties ingredients to make extra patties for the freezer. Using ground flax seed in the sausage patties makes them gluten free."

Sausage Patties

1.5 pounds (680g) ground pork
2 tablespoons breadcrumbs (or ground flax seed)
1.5 tablespoons beaten egg
1.5 tablespoons red wine vinegar
2 teaspoons dried parsley
1.5 teaspoons salt
1.5 teaspoons ground black pepper
1.5 teaspoons garlic powder
1.5 teaspoons onion powder
1.5 teaspoons dried basil
1.5 teaspoons fennel seed, ground
1 teaspoon smoked paprika
1 teaspoon red pepper flakes, optional
1 teaspoon brown sugar
1/2 teaspoon dried oregano
1/2 teaspoon dried thyme

Other ingredients

6 English Muffins
Butter
Slices of old cheddar (enough to cover 6 halves of the English Muffins)
6 large eggs

1. Add all of the sausage patties ingredients to a medium mixing bowl. Combine by hand thoroughly until completely mixed. Form 6 equally sized patties (approximately 130g each, 4 inches in diameter, 1/4 inch thick) and place them on a parchment lined baking sheet.
2. Toast the English muffins and butter them. Place slices of cheddar on one half of each English muffin.

3. Fry the 6 sausage patties over medium to medium-low heat until browned and cooked through (internal temp should be minimum 71° Celsius or 160° Fahrenheit), approximately 5 to 6 minutes per side. Place each sausage patty on the cheese covered halves of the English Muffins.
4. Fry or poach the 6 eggs to your desired doneness and place on top of the cooked sausage patties.
5. For presentation, place the top buttered halves of the English muffins off-kilter on the edge of the finished halves (with the cheese, sausage, egg) so you can see more of the egg on top.

Makes 6 breakfast sandwiches

Toad in the Hole

"A classic British dish. Basically, a big Yorkshire pudding with sausages in it...with a funny name! Traditionally served with red onion gravy, but I also like this served with maple syrup instead of the gravy. Good for breakfast, lunch, or dinner – you choose!"

1 tablespoon canola oil
5 sausages, 100g each (I use Bangers)
4 eggs, beaten
1.5 cups milk
1.5 cups all-purpose flour
4 tablespoons sugar
1.5 teaspoons salt

1. Preheat oven to 425°F.
2. Add the oil to an 8x11-inch baking dish. Add the sausages to the baking dish and rotate them in the oil and use the sausages to spread the oil all over the bottom of the baking dish.
3. Bake the sausages for 10 minutes, turning them once at the 5-minute mark.
4. Meanwhile whisk the eggs and the milk together. Add the flour, sugar, and salt and continue whisking until fully combined.
5. After the sausages have baked for 10 minutes, quickly pour this batter in the baking dish with the sausages and get it back in the oven (making sure that the sausages are evenly spaced.
6. Bake for 30 minutes until golden brown and puffed up. Do not open the oven during the baking process or it will deflate.
7. Serve immediately at the table. It will deflate as it sits (this is normal).
8. Serve with drizzles of maple syrup OR red onion gravy (recipe below).

Makes 10 small portions

Red Onion Gravy

3 tablespoons butter, separated
1.5 cups thinly sliced red onion (1 medium/large red onion)
1/2 teaspoon salt
2 tablespoons all-purpose flour

2 cups beef broth
1/2 teaspoon sugar

1. Heat a pan over medium heat for 1 minute.
2. Melt 2 tablespoons of the butter until foamy. Stir in the onion and salt. Cook for 10 minutes, stirring occasionally, until the onion slices are soft and they begin to caramelize.
3. Stir in the remaining 1 tablespoon of butter and the flour. Cook for 2 minutes stirring frequently.
4. Gradually stir the beef broth until fully combined. Add the sugar. Bring to a boil over high heat, and then turn the heat down to medium-high and continue to cook, stirring frequently, until desired consistency is reached, about 2 minutes.

Makes approximately 2 cups of gravy

Sausage, Tomato & Herb Frittata

"Using sundried tomatoes, instead of fresh tomatoes, offer more robust flavour. Also use true Italian Parmigiano Reggiano as your parmesan cheese of choice."

2 tablespoons extra virgin olive oil
500g mild Italian sausages, removed from casings
1 medium onion, diced small
6 garlic cloves, minced
1 cup oil packed sundried tomatoes, drained and finely chopped
1/4 cup finely chopped fresh basil
1/4 cup finely chopped fresh oregano
2 teaspoons salt
1/2 teaspoon pepper
12 large eggs
1.25 cups grated Parmigiano Reggiano
Sour cream, optional

1. Preheat the oven to 350°F and prepare a 10-inch round baking dish by spraying it with baking spray.
2. Add olive oil, sausage meat, onion and garlic to a frying pan and cook over medium heat for approximately 10 to 15 minutes until the sausage meat is cooked and the onion and garlic are soft. Stir occasionally breaking up the sausage meat into small bits as it cooks.
3. Transfer cooked sausage mixture to a large mixing bowl. Add the sundried tomatoes, basil, oregano, salt, pepper, eggs, and 3/4 cup of the grated parmesan cheese. Combine thoroughly together.
4. Pour the mixture into the prepared pan and take care to spread evenly. Top evenly with the remaining 1/2 cup of parmesan cheese. Bake for approximately 45 to 50 minutes until firm and lightly browned. The center of the frittata should not jiggle.
5. Remove from the oven and let stand on a cooling rack for at least 15 minutes before cutting and serving. Optional: serve with dollops of sour cream.

Makes 8 to 12 Portions

RECIPE NOTES

SEAFOOD

Crab & Roasted Red Pepper Strata

Recipe Courtesy of BC Egg, bcegg.com

2 cans chunky crabmeat (120 g each), well-drained
1/2 cup chopped, drained canned roasted red peppers
4 green onions, sliced
4 tablespoons chopped fresh parsley, divided
2 teaspoons fresh thyme
10 slices whole grain bread, cut into 1/2-inch cubes
6 large eggs
1 tablespoon Dijon mustard
Pinch of ground nutmeg
1/4 to 1/2 teaspoon hot pepper sauce
2 cups milk
3 tablespoons freshly grated parmesan cheese
1 teaspoon paprika

1. Place crabmeat in a medium bowl. Pat roasted red peppers dry with paper towels and add to crabmeat, along with green onions, 2 tablespoons of the parsley, and the thyme. Combine well.
2. Place half of bread cubes in a shallow, greased 9 x 13-inch baking dish. Spoon crabmeat mixture over bread cubes. Top with remaining bread cubes.
3. Whisk together eggs, Dijon mustard, nutmeg, and hot pepper sauce.
4. Whisk in milk. Pour egg mixture evenly over top of bread cubes. Top with Parmesan cheese and sprinkle with paprika.
5. Cover and refrigerate overnight.
6. Remove from refrigerator and bake, uncovered at 350°F for 55 to 60 minutes or until a knife inserted in centre comes out clean. Sprinkle with remaining 2 tablespoons fresh parsley. Let stand for 5 minutes before serving.

Makes 8 portions

Cajun Shrimp Egg Salad Sandwiches

"A reinvention of a classic sandwich with the infusion of Cajun flavours and prawns, because life is too short to eat bland egg salad sandwiches"

300g raw prawns (16/20 size or smaller), peeled & deveined
1/3 cup minced onion
1 teaspoon smoked paprika
1/2 teaspoon dried oregano
1/2 teaspoon salt
1/2 teaspoon ground black pepper
1/4 teaspoon ground cayenne pepper
2 teaspoons canola oil, divided
3/4 cup mayonnaise
1/4 cup small diced celery
1/4 cup small diced red bell pepper
2 tablespoons finely chopped fresh chives
2 tablespoons sweet green relish
1 tablespoon dill pickle juice
1 teaspoon lemon juice
3 to 4 dashes Tabasco brand hot sauce
6 large, hard-boiled eggs, chilled, peeled, & rough chopped
Salt & pepper to season, if desired
4 – 4" brioche buns, cut in half horizontally

1. Cut the prawns into small pieces, if desired. Combine the prawns in a small bowl with the minced onion, paprika, oregano, 1/2 teaspoon salt, 1/2 teaspoon black pepper, cayenne pepper, and 1 teaspoon of the canola oil.

2. Heat a 10-inch non-stick frying pan over medium-high heat. Add the remaining 1 teaspoon of canola oil, and then the prawn mixture. Cook, stirring constantly, until the prawns are cooked through, approximately 2 minutes. Transfer this cooked prawn mixture to a shallow tray or dinner plate and refrigerate immediately to chill while you prepare the other ingredients.

3. In a medium mixing bowl, combine the mayonnaise, celery, bell pepper, chives, relish, pickle juice, lemon juice, and Tabasco together.

Stir in the chilled chopped hard-boiled eggs, and the chilled prawn mixture. Season to taste with salt & pepper, if desired.
4. Portion mixture equally onto the 4 prepared buns and serve immediately.

Makes 4 sandwiches (approximately 3 cups of egg salad mixture)

Pastry Wrapped Wild Mushroom Halibut

"If fresh halibut filets are not available, use frozen – just thaw and pat them dry with paper towel."

2 tablespoons butter
1/2 medium onion, diced small
6 garlic cloves, minced
Salt & pepper
1-pound (454g) mixed variety of mushrooms, sliced
- preferably portabella, shitake, & oyster mushrooms
1/4 cup white wine
1/2 cup whipping cream
1 teaspoon sugar
2 pounds fresh, boneless halibut filets
2 – 397g pkgs of frozen puff pastry, thawed & chilled
All-purpose flour
1 large egg, mixed with 1 tablespoon water
Lots of fresh chives
1 lemon

1. Preheat oven to 400°F.
2. Over medium heat, melt butter in a large non-stick pan.
3. Add the onions, garlic, and season with salt & pepper. Cook until soft, approximately 2 to 3 minutes, stirring occasionally.
4. Add the sliced mushrooms and the white wine. Season with more salt & pepper. Turn the heat to medium-high and cook until soft, approximately 3 minutes, stirring occasionally.
5. Stir in the whipping cream and sugar. Taste & re-season if necessary, and remove from the heat.
6. Cut the fish into 6 equal portions and lightly season both sides with salt & pepper.
7. Cut pastry into 6 equal portions. On a lightly floured surface, roll out pastry portions into rectangles large enough to enclose each piece of fish.

8. Place each piece of fish on a portion of pastry and top each one with 1/6 of the mushroom mixture, approximately 3 to 4 tablespoons. Add 2 sprigs of chives, chopped to each portion.
9. With a pastry brush, moisten all the edges of the pastry with egg wash. Enclose each portion by folding up the sides and tucking underneath to completely enclose the halibut pieces.
10. Place pastry packets on a parchment paper lined baking sheet and bake for 25 minutes until golden brown.
11. Garnish each portion with a twist of lemon and chopped fresh chives.

Makes 6 portions

West Coast Cauliflower Kedgeree

"A Kedgeree is a curried rice dish from the UK and is classically made with smoked haddock and boiled eggs. We have replaced the traditional rice, with cauliflower rice and used smoked salmon instead of the haddock."

4 large eggs, hardboiled, cooled
1 large head of cauliflower
2 tablespoons of avocado oil, or canola oil
1 medium onion, diced small
3 cloves of garlic, minced
2 teaspoons grated fresh ginger
3 teaspoons curry powder
2 teaspoons salt
1 teaspoon ground turmeric
1/2 teaspoon ground pepper
1 cup frozen peas
175 grams smoked salmon, broken into bite sized chunks
Chopped fresh parsley, for garnish
Lemon wedges, for serving

1. Peel the hardboiled eggs and cut them into quarters. Set aside.
2. Rice the cauliflower by grating the florets with a cheese grater, or by pulsing in a food processor to transform into rice looking granules, about 6 cups. Set aside.
3. Heat a large skillet over medium heat. Add the oil, then the onion, garlic, ginger, curry powder, salt, turmeric and pepper. Stir to combine and cook until soft and fragrant, approximately 2 to 3 minutes, stirring occasionally.
4. Stir in the frozen peas and cook for another minute.
5. Turn the heat to medium-high and add the reserved cauliflower rice from step 2. Cook while stirring constantly for approximately 3 to 4 minutes. It is important to use a large skillet over higher heat so that the cauliflower granules stay more separate and don't become mushy (the larger pan and higher heat will evaporate any moisture that comes out of the cauliflower).

6. Turn off the heat and stir in the chunks of smoked salmon. Portion into dishes while garnishing equally with the quartered eggs and some parsley. Serve with lemon wedges.

Makes 7 cups

VEGETARIAN

Breakfast Power Bowl

Recipe Courtesy of BC Egg, bcegg.com

1 tablespoon white vinegar
4 large eggs
4 tablespoons olive oil, divided
1 clove garlic, minced
6 cups fresh baby spinach
1 teaspoon salt, divided
1 teaspoon pepper, divided
1 cup quinoa, cooked to desired doneness
1 tablespoon lemon juice
1 ripe avocado, peeled, pitted and chopped
1/4 cup crumbled goat cheese
2 tablespoons toasted pumpkin seeds

1. Fill a pan with enough water to come 3 inches up the side; heat to gentle simmer. Stir in vinegar. Break cold egg into small dish or saucer. Holding dish just above simmering water, gently slip egg into water; repeat with remaining eggs. Cook in barely simmering water for 3 to 5 minutes or until whites are set and yolks are cooked as desired. Remove eggs with slotted spoon. Drain on paper towel and set aside.
2. Heat 2 tablespoons of the oil in a skillet set over medium heat; cook garlic for about 1 minute or until fragrant. Add spinach; cook for 2 to 3 minutes or until starting to wilt. Season with 1/2 teaspoon salt and 1/2 teaspoon pepper.
3. Toss together the cooked quinoa, lemon juice and remaining 2 tablespoons olive oil; divide evenly among 4 bowls. Top with cooked spinach, avocado, goat cheese and pumpkin seeds. Top with poached eggs. Season with remaining salt and pepper.

Makes 4 portions

Breakfast Tostadas

Recipe Courtesy of BC Egg, bcegg.com

"Add pickled jalapeño or serve with hot sauce to add some kick to this dish"

4 large eggs
4 tostadas
1/2 cup refried beans
1/2 cup grated cheddar cheese
1/2 cup salsa
1/4 cup sour cream
1/2 avocado, sliced
2 tablespoons chopped fresh cilantro
2 tablespoons chopped green onion

1. Set a large non-stick skillet over medium heat, grease well with non-stick cooking spray. Crack eggs into skillet. Cook for 3 minutes for sunny-side up or until desired doneness is achieved.
2. Meanwhile, preheat broiler to high. Arrange tostadas on parchment-lined baking sheet. Spread refried beans over tostadas and sprinkle with cheese. Broil for 2 to 3 minutes or until cheese is melted.
3. Slide each egg onto tostada. Top with salsa, sour cream, avocado, cilantro and green onion. Serve immediately.

Makes 4 portions

Caramelized Onion & Artichoke Frittata

"Great for brunch, lunch, or dinner. The bake time will depend on the temperature of your raw eggs: room temperature eggs will yield a bake time closer to the 17-minute mark, and cold eggs directly from the fridge will yield a bake time closer to the 22-minute mark."

2 tablespoons butter
2 large sweet onions (or yellow onions), thinly sliced (about 6 cups sliced)
1 tablespoon balsamic vinegar
1 tablespoon dark brown sugar
2.5 teaspoons salt, divided

1/2 teaspoon dried thyme leaves (not ground thyme)
8 large eggs
1/4 cup milk
2 tablespoons Dijon mustard
1/2 teaspoon smoked paprika
1/2 teaspoon ground black pepper
398ml (13.5oz) can of artichoke hearts, drained and quartered
1 cup grated smoked gouda cheese
Extra smoked paprika for sprinkling
Sour cream for serving, optional
Fresh thyme sprigs, for garnish, optional

1. Preheat oven to 400°F.
2. Heat a 10-inch cast iron skillet over medium heat. Add the butter and once the butter is melted and foaming, stir in the onions, balsamic, brown sugar, 1.5 teaspoons of the salt, and the dried thyme.
3. Cook over medium heat, stirring occasionally, until the onions are soft and just starting to brown, approximately 15 minutes.
4. Reduce heat to low and continue to cook, stirring occasionally, until the onions have reduced and become caramelized, approximately 15 more minutes.
5. In a mixing bowl, beat the eggs, milk, Dijon mustard, the remaining 1 teaspoon of salt, paprika, and pepper together thoroughly. Smooth the onions out to level them in the pan and then pour this egg mixture into the pan over the onions. Arrange the quartered artichoke hearts in the egg mixture, top evenly with the grated cheese, and sprinkle a little more smoked paprika on top.
6. Transfer the skillet to the preheated oven and bake for approximately 17 to 22 minutes until the eggs are set (check by making a small cut in the center; the eggs should not be runny), and the top has browned.
7. Remove from the oven and let cool in the pan for at least 5 minutes. Cut into 8 equal pie shaped pieces and serve each piece with a dollop of sour cream and garnished with a sprig of fresh thyme, or a sprinkle of fresh thyme leaves

Makes 8 portions

Cheese Soufflés with Creamy Leek Sauce

"Soufflés are not as difficult as some people think, and this makes a wonderful treat. Baking time will depend on the temperature of your raw eggs. The finished soufflés will deflate a bit as they sit, but this is normal."

Soufflés
Butter for ramekins
1/3 cup finely ground parmesan cheese
3 tablespoons butter
3 tablespoons flour
1 teaspoon Dijon mustard
3/4 teaspoon salt
1/4 teaspoon ground cayenne pepper
1 cup milk
100g grated aged cheddar cheese
6 large eggs, yolks separated from whites
1 teaspoon sugar

Creamy Leek Sauce
2 tablespoons butter
1 leek, white part only, halved and sliced thin, about 1 cup packed
1 cup whipping cream
3/4 teaspoon salt
1/4 teaspoon pepper

1. Preheat oven to 375°F.
2. Prepare five 1-cup sized (250ml) oven safe ramekins by buttering them and then dusting them with the finely ground parmesan thoroughly; tapping out any excess. After coating all five ramekins, if there is any parmesan left, add it to the grated cheddar.
3. Melt the 3 tablespoons of butter in a medium pot over medium heat. Stir in the flour and reduce the heat to medium/low. Cook for about 2 to 3 minutes to remove the starchy taste of the flour, stirring occasionally.
4. Stir in the mustard, 3/4 teaspoon salt, and cayenne. Slowly whisk in the milk to ensure no lumps, until fully combined. Turn the heat to

medium and wait until the mixture just starts to boil to thicken a bit, stirring occasionally.

5. Take the pot off the heat and stir in the grated cheddar until fully melted and combined.

6. Transfer this milk/cheese mixture to a large mixing bowl and let stand for 5 minutes to cool a bit. Then stir in the egg yolks, one at a time, to this mixture.

7. Beat the egg whites in a stand mixture with whisk attachment until foamy, then add the 1 teaspoon of sugar. With the sugar added, beat the egg whites on high speed until stiff peaks form. Stir approximately 1/3 of these whipped egg whites into the cheese mixture. Gently fold in the remaining egg whites thoroughly.

8. Pour the soufflé mixture equally into the prepared ramekins. Once filled, tap them on the counter a few times to knock out any air bubbles. Place the filled ramekins on a baking sheet and bake in the oven for approximately 17 to 20 minutes (depending on the temperature of your eggs), until puffed up, set and cracked on top.

9. While the soufflés are baking, prepare the leek sauce: Melt 2 tablespoons of butter in a medium pan over medium heat. Add the sliced leeks and cook, stirring occasionally, until soft, about 2 to 3 minutes. Stir in the whipping cream and season with the salt and pepper. Then bring to a boil, and then reduce until thickened a bit, about 2 minutes. Remove from heat.

10. Put each hot ramekin on a serving plate and top with equal amounts of the leek sauce. Alternatively, you can let them cool a bit and then garnish with the sauce to serve, just keep in mind that the soufflés will deflate a bit as they sit but they are still excellent.

Makes 5 portions

 Do you know the difference between white eggs and brown? It's simply the colour of the hen that lays them!

Easy Egg Quesadillas – makes 2 portions

2 large eggs, beaten
Salt
Chili powder
2 large flour tortillas
1.5 cups grated cheddar
1/2 red bell pepper, diced small
2 to 4 tablespoons chopped pickled jalapenos
Salsa and sour cream for serving, optional

1. Cook the beaten eggs in a non-stick pan with a sprinkle of salt and chili powder, until you have cooked scrambled eggs. Set aside.
2. Preheat a griddle or 2 large pans over medium to medium-high heat. Place the 2 tortillas on the heated cooking surface and sprinkle the grated cheese equally all over the tortillas (3/4 cup cheese for each tortilla).
3. Once the cheese has melted, season the tortillas with a sprinkle of salt and chili powder. Then on one half of each of the tortillas, equally arrange the reserved scrambled eggs, bell pepper, and pickled jalapenos. Fold the uncovered halves of the tortillas over the covered halves and cook until both sides are lightly browned and moderately crispy, approximately 3 to 6 minutes.
4. Cut each tortilla into 4 triangle shaped pieces and serve with the optional salsa and sour cream.

Egg & Quinoa Power Bowls

"The idea of this meal is to try and keep it as healthy as possible and filling the hunger gap with powerful nutrients. Because of this I recommend using extra virgin avocado oil and raw unfiltered apple cider vinegar, but extra virgin olive oil and regular apple cider vinegar can be substituted if desired. Also, important to note that the blueberries play a key role in providing sweetness to balance the dressing and the overall dish."

2 cups vegetable broth
1 cup dry quinoa (white, red, or black, or a combination totalling 1 cup)
1/2 teaspoon salt

4 baby sweet red peppers, sliced (or 2 cups chopped red bell peppers)
540ml can chickpeas, drained, and rinsed
2 cups shredded cabbage
40 grape tomatoes
4 mini cucumbers, sliced (or 2 cups sliced cucumbers)
4 large, hard-boiled eggs, peeled (sliced in halves or chopped)
Handful of fresh baby spinach leaves, sliced thin
1/2 small red onion, sliced thin
1 cup walnut halves
2 cups fresh blueberries (or thawed, drained from frozen)
Kosher salt (or other pure finishing salt), to season
Fresh cracked pepper, to season

Dressing
6 tablespoons extra virgin avocado oil
1/4 cup raw unfiltered apple cider vinegar
2 tablespoons whole grain mustard (seed mustard)

1. Put vegetable broth, 1 cup quinoa, and 1/2 teaspoon salt in a medium pot. Bring to a boil over high heat, then turn down to medium-low heat and cook uncovered until all the broth is gone, stirring occasionally. Remove from heat and chill or keep at room temperature.
2. In 4 large diameter shallow bowls, arrange equal amounts of the following in each of the 4 bowls starting with the quinoa and working clockwise: cooked quinoa, sweet red peppers, chickpeas, cabbage, grape tomatoes, and cucumbers. The bottom of the bowl should be completely covered with these ingredients.
3. Arrange the following ingredients in equal amounts on top of the ingredients from step 2: eggs, spinach, red onion, walnuts, blueberries, kosher salt, and fresh cracked pepper.
4. Combine the dressing ingredients (extra virgin avocado oil, apple cider vinegar, mustard) together thoroughly. Drizzle 3 tablespoons of this dressing on each portion.

Makes 4 large portions or 6 smaller portions

Eggs Makhani

Recipe Courtesy of BC Egg, bcegg.com

"Eggs Makhani is a dish from North India, similar to butter chicken but with eggs as the star. It's a thick, creamy, mild curry and is best served with rice or naan."

3 tablespoon canola oil or vegetable oil
4 black peppercorns
4 green cardamom pods
1/4 cup chickpea flour (besan)
1/4 cup canned crushed tomatoes
1/2 teaspoon garlic paste
1/4 teaspoon ginger paste
2 teaspoons white sugar
1 teaspoon ground coriander
1/2 teaspoon ground cumin
1/2 teaspoon ground turmeric
1/4 teaspoon chilli powder
1/2 teaspoon salt (or to taste)
1.25 cups water, divided
1/3 cup half-and-half (10%MF) cream
4 hard-boiled eggs, peeled, cut in half lengthwise
1/2 teaspoon garam masala, to garnish
2 tablespoons finely chopped fresh cilantro

1. In a medium heavy-based pan, heat oil on medium-high. Add peppercorns and cardamom and fry for one minute. Add chickpea flour and stir constantly for a couple of minutes until golden brown in colour.
2. Mix in crushed tomatoes and then the garlic paste ginger paste, sugar, coriander, cumin, turmeric, chilli powder, and salt. Cook for a couple minutes.
3. Add 1 cup of the water to create a smooth sauce. Whisk if necessary to remove any lumps. Simmer for a couple more minutes on medium heat.
4. Stir in cream and add the remaining 1/4 cup of water to thin out the sauce. Gently add the hard-boiled eggs and coat with the sauce.

Simmer for a couple minutes. Garnish with a sprinkle of garam masala and cilantro. Serve with basmati rice and naan.

Makes 4 portions

Huevos Divorciados

Recipe Courtesy of Sean Bromilow, diversivore.com

"A classic play on the ever-popular huevos rancheros, this Mexican dish features two eggs with fried tortillas, served with two separate ("divorced") salsas."

2 corn tortillas
2 teaspoons vegetable oil
2 large eggs
Pinch of salt
2 tablespoons salsa roja (red salsa) homemade or store-bought
2 tablespoons salsa verde (green salsa) homemade or store-bought 1/4 cup refried Beans, optional
Cotija or queso fresco, optional
Chopped fresh cilantro, optional

1. Preheat a skillet over medium heat. Add a tortilla and fry one side for 30-45 seconds, or until it's a little toasted and nicely flexible. Flip the tortilla and fry for another 20 seconds, then set it aside on the serving plate and repeat the process with the second tortilla.
2. Increase the heat to high and add the vegetable oil. Add the eggs to the hot pan, season with salt, and fry to desired doneness. For this recipe, I like a soft yolk and firm whites, so I let the bottoms crisp up in the oil, then cover the pan with a lid for 30 seconds or so to finish firming up the whites.
3. Plate the finished eggs on the tortillas. Top one egg with salsa roja, and one with salsa verde. If you're using refried beans, you can serve them on the side, or make a little partition between the two eggs for added drama. Top with cotija or queso fresco and a sprinkling of cilantro.

Makes 1 portion

Goat Cheese Strata with Peppers & Onions

Recipe Courtesy of Sean Bromilow, diversivore.com – Makes 8 portions

"Bready, cheesy, eggy goodness with a more 'grown-up' dinnertime spin! This crowd-pleasing vegetarian strata recipe features big, bold French flavours, while being easy to make ahead of time."

1 tablespoon butter
2 red bell peppers, chopped
1 medium onion, chopped
2 cloves garlic, minced
1/2 cup red wine
Butter for the baking tray
4 cups crusty whole wheat bread (325 g) cut into cubes
100g goat cheese, crumbled
100g grated Emmental cheese (or Swiss, Gruyere, Fontina)
6 extra-large eggs or 7 large eggs
2 cups milk
1/2 teaspoon salt
1/8 teaspoon ground black pepper
Pinch dried thyme
Fresh oregano to garnish, optional

1. Melt the butter in a skillet over medium heat. Add the peppers, onions, and a pinch of salt, and sauté for 5 minutes. Add the garlic and red wine and cook for an additional 5 minutes. Set aside to cool.
2. Butter an 8x8 baking tray, then layer it with the bread cubes. (See the notes below if you want to prepare this the night before).
3. Scatter crumbled and grated cheeses over the bread, reserving a bit to sprinkle on top at the end. I like to toss the bread cubes a bit to mix the cheese in a little more.
4. Scatter the reserved cooked peppers and onions over the bread and cheese.
5. Combine eggs, milk, salt, pepper, and thyme. Whisk together thoroughly, then pour over the bread/cheese/veggies. If necessary, gently press the bread down to make sure that it sinks into the liquid. Let stand for 30 minutes on the counter.

6. Preheat oven to 350°F, bake for 45-50 minutes, or until the egg is just set and no longer jiggly in the center. Finish the strata under the broiler to brown and crisp up the surface (2-3 minutes but keep an eye on it).

NOTES

Make-ahead option - Strata can be put together ahead the day before and baked when you want them ready, but you do need to add an extra step to keep the bread from becoming too soggy in the eggs. Simply scatter the cut bread pieces on a baking tray and bake in a low oven (about 250°F) for 20 minutes, or until the bread cubes are dry and a little browned. Once this is done, you can continue with the remaining steps as written above.

Bake and freeze option - Once baked and cooled, your strata can be refrigerated for 2 to 3 days or frozen for 3+ months. Refrigerated or frozen strata is best warmed up in a low oven. You can microwave individual portions too, but make sure to do so carefully and in small time increments, or you might find that the eggy portion has a tendency to explode and make a disaster out of your microwave.

Muffin Tin Frittatas – Makes 12 small portions
Recipe Courtesy of BC Egg, bcegg.com

8 large eggs
1/2 cup milk
1/4 teaspoon salt
1/4 teaspoon pepper
1 cup grated Monterey Jack cheese
2 green onions, thinly sliced
1/2 cup salsa

1. Preheat oven to 375°F. Grease 12-cup muffin tin; set aside.
2. Whisk together eggs, milk, salt, and pepper.
3. Stir in cheese and green onions; divide evenly among muffin cups. Bake until eggs are set, approximately 12 to 15 minutes.
4. Run thin knife around edge of each cup and remove frittatas. Let cool for 5 minutes or serve at room temperature. To serve, top with salsa.

Indian Spiced Rice & Eggs
Recipe Courtesy of BC Egg, bcegg.com

2 tablespoons butter
1 red onion, diced
1 clove garlic, minced
1 red bell pepper, seeded and diced
1 tablespoon curry powder (mild or hot)
1 cup basmati rice
1.75 cups vegetable stock or water
1 tablespoon white vinegar
4 large eggs
1 cup baby spinach leaves
1/4 cup chopped fresh mint
Salt and pepper

1. In a large saucepan, melt butter over medium heat. Add onion and cook until transparent (about 2 minutes), stirring frequently. Add garlic and cook for 1 minute, stirring frequently. Add red pepper and curry powder; stir to combine. Add rice and stir for 1 minute. Add stock, stir, and bring to a boil. Once boiling, reduce heat to low. Cover and cook for 15 minutes.

2. Meanwhile, while rice is cooking, fill a medium saucepan with 3 to 4 inches of water. Add vinegar and bring to a boil. Reduce heat to simmer. Break each egg into a small ramekin or bowl. Gently slide eggs into simmering water one at a time. Cook until whites are set and yolks are soft, 3 to 4 minutes (3 minutes makes a runnier egg). Remove eggs with a slotted spoon.

3. Once rice is cooked, remove from heat, uncover, and fluff with a fork. Stir in spinach and mint, season with salt and pepper. Divide rice onto four plates. Place an egg on top of each bed of spiced rice.

Makes 4 portions

Shakshuka – Makes 4 portions

Recipe Courtesy of BC Egg, bcegg.com

"Substitute goat cheese for feta cheese and chopped mint for parsley if desired"

3 tablespoons olive oil
1 small onion, chopped
1 red bell pepper, chopped
4 garlic cloves, minced
3 tablespoons tomato paste
2 teaspoons ground cumin
1 teaspoon ground coriander
1 teaspoon smoked paprika
1/2 teaspoon salt
1/4 teaspoon cinnamon
1/4 teaspoon hot pepper flakes
1/4 teaspoon freshly ground pepper
796ml can diced tomatoes
8 large eggs
1/4 cup finely crumbled feta cheese
2 tablespoons chopped fresh parsley
4 Greek-style pitas (7 inch/18 cm), toasted

1. Preheat oven to 400°F. In a large ovenproof high-sided skillet, heat oil over medium heat; cook onion, bell pepper, garlic, tomato paste, cumin, coriander, paprika, salt, cinnamon, hot pepper flakes, and pepper, stirring occasionally, until vegetables start to soften and tomato paste is deep red and very fragrant, approximately 3 to 5 minutes.
2. Add diced tomatoes to skillet; cook, stirring occasionally, until thickened, approximately 10 minutes.
3. Reduce heat to medium-low. Using a spoon, make 8 divots in the sauce mixture and crack 1 egg into each divot.
4. Baste each egg with a little of the tomato sauce and transfer to the oven. Bake until egg whites are set but yolks are still soft, or until eggs are cooked to desired doneness, approximately 8 to 10 minutes. Garnish with feta and parsley. Serve with pita bread.

Mediterranean Creamy Baked Eggs

"If you are looking for the perfect brunch idea – this is it! Eggs baked in individual ramekins in an array of Mediterranean flavours and cream."

1/4 cup oil-packed sundried tomatoes, oil drained, reserved, and divided
100g fresh baby spinach, approximately 2 cups packed
1/2 cup finely grated Parmigiano-Reggiano cheese, divided
4 tablespoons prepared basil pesto (store bought or homemade)
8 tablespoons whipping cream
4 large eggs
Sprinkle of salt & fresh cracked pepper
Sprinkle of ground sumac*, optional
Bread, cut into "fingers", toasted & buttered, optional

1. Preheat oven to 350°F and arrange four 1-cup oven-safe ramekins in cake pan that will just hold all four ramekins.
2. Measure 1/2 teaspoon of the reserved oil (from the sundried tomatoes) into each of the 4 ramekins and coat the inside of each ramekin thoroughly.
3. Place a non-stick pan over medium-high heat. Add the remaining reserved oil to the pan and sauté the spinach until completely wilted and cooked down, about 1 minute, stirring constantly. Divide this cooked spinach equally into the four prepared ramekins.
4. Sprinkle 1 tablespoon of the cheese into each of the ramekins on top of the spinach.
5. Distribute 1 tablespoon of pesto into each of the ramekins.
6. Divide the reserved sundried tomatoes equally into the ramekins.
7. Pour 2 tablespoons of whipping cream into each of the ramekins.
8. Crack 1 egg into each of the ramekins, taking care to not break the yolks.
9. Top each ramekin equally with the remaining cheese, a sprinkle of salt & pepper, and a sprinkle of sumac.
10. Pour boiling water from a kettle into the cake pan (to make a bain-marie) until the water is at least halfway up the outer sides of the ramekins.

11. Carefully transport to the oven and bake for 15 to 20 minutes until the whites of the eggs are cooked but the yolks are still runny.
12. Carefully remove each ramekin, and serve with the optional toasted bread, or just simply serve with spoons.

Makes 4 portions

*Sumac is a wine-coloured ground spice with a distinct citrusy tartness. It is most prevalent in the middle east but also popular in a lot of Mediterranean regions.

Sheet Pan Eggs – makes 6 portions
"Normally a recipe like this would use a standard jelly roll pan (12x17 inches), but I prefer to do this in a smaller toaster oven pan instead (9x11 inches). Great as a brunch item or to replace meat in a sandwich."

Baking spray
Parchment paper
9 large eggs
3 tablespoons milk
1.5 teaspoons salt
3/4 teaspoon ground black pepper
1/2 cup grated cheddar cheese
Sprinkle of smoked paprika

1. Preheat your oven or toaster oven to 375°F.
2. Spray a 9x11 inch toaster oven pan with baking spray. Line with parchment paper (make sure there is enough parchment up the sides of the pan too) and spray the parchment with baking spray.
3. In a mixing bowl, whisk the eggs, milk, salt, and pepper together until completely homogenized. Pour this mixture into the prepared pan.
4. Top evenly with the grated cheese and bake for approximately 12 to 15 minutes until the eggs have become firm or reached an internal temperature of at least 160°F.
5. Cut to desired size pieces and serve immediately.

Smoky Stuffed Sweet Potatoes

"Orange fleshed sweet potatoes are packed full of nutrition just like BC Eggs! Pairing them together with smoked gouda and sweet smoked paprika makes this dish extra delicious."

2 large orange sweet potatoes, approximately 800g each, baked and cooled
10 fresh spinach leaves, chopped
1/4 cup sliced sun-dried tomatoes, packed in oil, drained
1/2 cup finely grated smoked gouda, divided into 2 parts
4 large BC eggs
1.5 tablespoons milk
1.5 teaspoons sweet smoked paprika
1.5 teaspoons salt
1/2 teaspoon pepper

1. Preheat oven to 375°F.
2. Cut the cold sweet potatoes in half lengthwise and carefully scoop out the centers, leaving approximately a 1/2-inch border of sweet potato left around the edges and bottoms. Be careful not to scoop all the way down to the skin otherwise your potato halves will not hold the egg mixture like a vessel. Placed them on a parchment lined baking sheet.
3. In each of the 4 prepared halves, divide and sprinkle equal amounts of the spinach, sun-dried tomatoes, and 1/4 cup of the smoked gouda.
4. In a medium bowl, whisk the eggs, milk, smoked paprika, salt, and pepper thoroughly together.
5. Carefully ladle this egg mixture into the prepared halves of sweet potato.
6. Sprinkle the remaining 1/4 cup smoked gouda over the filled halves.
7. Bake for 15 to 20 minutes until the egg mixture has set.
8. Turn the oven to broil, and place under the broiler until just browned a bit, 1 to 2 minutes.
9. Let cool for about 10 to 20 minutes before serving.

Makes 4 large portions

Sweet Potato Spinach Patties

500g orange sweet potato, peeled, diced 1/2 inch
300g package frozen chopped spinach, thawed and drained by squeezing
100g feta cheese, finely crumbled
2 large eggs
2/3 cup cornflake crumbs
2 large garlic cloves, pressed into a paste
1.5 teaspoons salt
1 teaspoon smoked paprika
1/2 teaspoon ground black pepper
2 teaspoons canola oil
6 tablespoons red pepper jelly
6 tablespoons sour cream
Finely chopped fresh chives

1. Steam the sweet potato for 15 - 20 minutes until tender. Let cool to room temperature in a large bowl.
2. Add the spinach, feta, eggs, cornflake crumbs, garlic, salt, paprika and pepper to the sweet potato and mix thoroughly.
3. Divide into 6 equal amounts and press into round (1/2 inch thick) patties.
4. Heat a large nonstick frying pan over medium heat. Drizzle pan with the canola oil. Fry patties for approximately 6 or 7 minutes per side until browned.
5. Serve each patty garnished by spreading 1 tablespoon pepper jelly, a dollop of 1 tablespoon sour cream, and a sprinkle of chopped chives.

Makes 6 portions

CAKES & PUDDINGS

Angel Food Cake

Recipe Courtesy of BC Egg, bcegg.com

1.25 cups sifted cake and pastry flour
1.5 cups granulated white sugar, divided
1/4 teaspoon salt
1.75 cups egg whites (13 to 15 egg whites), at room temperature
1.5 teaspoons cream of tartar
1 teaspoon vanilla extract

1. Preheat oven to 350°F.
2. Stir together flour, 3/4 cup of the sugar, and the salt until well blended. Set aside.
3. Beat the egg whites in large stainless steel or glass bowl with electric mixer on low until frothy. Add cream of tartar and beat on high speed until soft peaks form. Add the remaining 3/4 cup sugar, about 1 tablespoon at a time, beating until sugar is dissolved, mixture is glossy and stiff peaks form. Beat in the vanilla. Sift flour mixture over egg white mixture in four parts, gently folding until just blended after each addition.
4. Spoon batter into ungreased 10-inch (4 litre) tube pan. Smooth the batter, then cut through in zig zag motion with knife to break up any air pockets; smooth top.
5. Bake in bottom third of oven until cake is golden brown and top springs back when gently pressed, about 30 minutes.
6. Remove from oven and immediately invert cake pan; if pan does not have legs, rest tube opening on neck of bottle or funnel or on bottom of glass or can. Cool upside down for a couple of hours.
7. When cake is cool, run thin spatula or knife around side of pan and centre tube to loosen cake. Invert cake onto serving plate. To serve, cut cake with scrrated knife.

Makes 16 portions

Blueberry-Juniper Rye Cake with Blueberry Curd

Recipe Courtesy of Sean Bromilow, diversivore.com

Cake

1.5 cups dark (whole grain) rye flour
1 cup all-purpose flour
1.25 cups white sugar
1 tablespoon baking powder
1 teaspoon juniper berries, ground
1 teaspoon ground cinnamon
1 cup unsalted butter, softened
1 cup milk
2 large eggs
1.5 cups blueberries

Glaze

2 tablespoons white sugar
2 tablespoons water
1/2 teaspoon juniper berries, ground
1/4 teaspoon ground cinnamon

Blueberry Curd

1.5 cups blueberries
1/4 cup lemon juice
2 egg yolks
2 large eggs
3/4 cup white sugar
1/2 cup unsalted butter
2 teaspoons lemon zest

1. Preheat oven to 350°F (176°C). Lightly grease a large loaf tin or line it with parchment paper. You can also use 2 square or round cake tins, though make sure to adjust the cooking time.
2. In a large bowl, combine the rye flour, all-purpose flour, 1.25 cups white sugar, baking powder, ground juniper, and cinnamon. Cut in the

1 cup butter with a pastry mixer and stop once the butter has been cut into small pieces and the mixture looks like smallish crumbs.

3. Combine the milk and 2 eggs and add them to the large bowl containing the flour mixture. Stir until the whole mixture is moist and just combined.
4. Add the 1.5 cups blueberries to the batter and combine gently.
5. Pour the batter into the prepared tin(s) and bake for 75 to 85 minutes, or until a toothpick can pierce the center of the cake and emerge dry. Prepare the glaze while the cake bakes.
6. Brush glaze over the finished cake as soon as it comes out of the oven. Use all of the glaze by allowing it to soak in and brushing it on in several coats.
7. Let the finished cake cool, ideally overnight, but for at least 2 hours. Served with the blueberry curd.

NOTES

Glaze: Combine all of the glaze ingredients in a small saucepan and bring to a boil, then reduce to a low simmer. Simmer for 2 minutes then let the glaze stand for 10 to 15 minutes. Pour the glaze through a small strainer or cheesecloth in order to filter out the cinnamon and juniper pieces. Set the syrupy glaze aside to use when the cake is done baking.

Blueberry Curd: Place the 1.5 cups blueberries and lemon juice in a small saucepan and heat on the stovetop over low heat, stirring frequently to break up the blueberries and avoid scorching. If you have trouble getting enough liquid to release at first, you can add a splash of water. Continue to cook and stir until all the berries have cooked and burst, leaving you with a thick sauce, about 5 to 7 minutes. Allow this mixture to cool while you prepare the other curd ingredients. Combine this mixture along with the other curd ingredients in a powerful high-speed blender and process for 5 minutes at the highest speed setting. (No high-speed blender? Check out the notes below for variations). Allow the finished curd to cool slightly and open the blender carefully, then refrigerate for at least 1 hour.

Recipe Notes – continued on next page

Recipe Notes for Blueberry-Juniper Rye Cake (on previous page)

When preparing the curd, the blender instructions are the easiest and most effective way to go, but necessitates the use of a high-power/high-speed blender (e.g. a Vitamix). Blenders like this will combine the ingredients effectively while simultaneously cooking them with the heat of the blender. Low power blenders will not work the same way. If you don't have one of these blenders, there are other options listed below.

Food Processor Version: Prepare the blueberries and lemon juice as for the blender version. Combine the sugar and lemon zest, then cream them with the butter (use a food processor or mixer for this). Add the blueberry mixture and continue to mix, followed by the egg yolks and whole eggs, one at a time, mixing continually. Add the mixture to a small saucepan on a stovetop. Heat over a low flame, stirring continuously, until the curd has thickened and set (around 12 to 15 minutes). When finished remove from the heat and refrigerate for at least 1 hour.

Traditional Stovetop Version: Prepare the blueberries and lemon juice as for the blender version, cooking a little longer to really break down the fruit. Press this mixture through a mesh sieve to get out the bits of blueberry skin. Add the blueberry puree, lemon zest, and butter to a small saucepan on a stovetop. Heat over a low flame, stirring and mixing until the butter is well mixed and homogeneous. Remove from heat and allow to cool to low temperature. In a separate bowl, whisk together the eggs and egg yolks. When the blueberry/butter mixture is cool, return it to the stove over low heat and whisk in the eggs. Heat over a low flame, stirring continuously, until the curd has thickened and set (around 12-15 minutes). When finished remove from heat and refrigerate for at least 1 hour.

Makes 12 portions

Blueberry Bread Pudding – Makes 10 to 12 portions

1 pound (454g) French loaf
Butter for the pan
4 large eggs, beaten
1.25 cups white sugar
1 teaspoon vanilla extract
1 teaspoon ground cinnamon
1/4 teaspoon salt
Zest from 2 lemons, finely chopped
2 cups 10%MF cream (half and half)
2 cups milk
2 cups blueberries (fresh or thawed frozen)
Vanilla bean ice cream, optional
Fresh mint leaves for garnish, optional

1. Preheat oven to 400 degrees. Tear the French bread into approximate 1-inch to 2-inch chunks and spread evenly on a large baking sheet. Bake in the oven for 10 minutes, tossing the pieces around about halfway through. Remove from the oven and let sit while you prepare the rest of the pudding.
2. Decrease the oven temperature to 350 degrees and prepare a 9x13-inch baking dish by buttering it.
3. In a large bowl, combine the eggs, sugar, vanilla, cinnamon, salt, and the zest thoroughly. Whisk in the cream and milk. Add the toasted bread pieces and toss together thoroughly with your hands. Let sit for 10 minutes for the bread pieces to absorb.
4. Put one half of the custard-soaked bread mixture into the prepared baking dish and top with 1 cup of the blueberries. Add the remaining bread mixture (and scrape all liquid from the bowl) to the dish and top with the remaining 1 cup blueberries. Bake for approximately 45 minutes until the top browns and puffs up. Also, an inserted butter knife should come out clean.
5. Let sit for at least 10 to 15 minutes before serving warm with vanilla bean ice cream and garnished with sprigs of fresh mint.

Chocolate Cake - Recipe Courtesy of BC Egg, bcegg.com

Cake

1.75 cups all-purpose flour, sifted
3/4 cup cocoa powder, sifted
2 teaspoons instant espresso powder
1 teaspoon baking powder
1 teaspoon baking soda
3/4 teaspoon salt
1 cup unsalted butter, room temperature
1 & 2/3 cups white sugar
2 large eggs
2 teaspoons vanilla extract
1.5 cups buttermilk

Frosting

3/4 cup cold unsalted butter, cubed
8 oz (230 g) bittersweet (or semisweet) chocolate, melted and cooled
1/4 cup cocoa powder, sifted
1/4 teaspoon salt
3 cups icing sugar, sifted
1/3 cup milk

1. Preheat oven to 350°F. Grease and line two 9-inch (23 cm) round cake pans with parchment paper. Whisk together flour, cocoa powder, espresso powder, baking powder, baking soda and salt until combined; set aside.

2. Using an electric mixer, beat 1 cup butter with white sugar until light and fluffy; beat in eggs, one at a time, making sure each egg is fully incorporated before the next addition. Beat in vanilla.

3. With mixer on low, alternately add the flour mixture in 3 parts and buttermilk in 2 parts, starting and ending with flour mixture; scrape down the bowl as needed between additions.

4. Pour batter into prepared pans and smooth the tops. Bake until tester comes out clean when inserted into center, approximately 25 to 30 minutes. Transfer to rack; let cool completely.

5. Prepare the frosting by using an electric mixer. Beat 3/4 cup butter on high speed until light and creamy; beat in melted and cooled chocolate,

1/4 cup cocoa powder and 1/4 teaspoon salt until smooth. Beat in icing sugar. Stir in milk and beat until creamy. If frosting is too soft to spread, refrigerate for 5 to 10 minutes. Smear a little frosting on a serving plate to prevent the cake from sliding. Place the first cake in the centre of the plate and spread 1 cup of frosting on top. Top with second cake layer; frost the top and sides of cake with remaining frosting. Refrigerate cake for at least 2 hours before serving.

Chocolate Zucchini Cake – Makes 12 to 14 portions

Recipe Courtesy of BC Egg, bcegg.com

"You can also bake in a 9x13-inch baking pan at 350°F for 50-55 minutes"

1 cup all-purpose flour
3/4 cup whole wheat flour
1 cup brown sugar
2/3 cup unsweetened cocoa powder
1/4 cup ground flax seed
2 teaspoons baking soda
1 teaspoon baking powder
1/2 teaspoon salt
1 teaspoon ground cinnamon
4 large eggs
3/4 cup canola oil
3/4 cup unsweetened applesauce
3/4 cup chopped walnuts (optional)
3 cups grated zucchini

1. Preheat oven to 350°F. Grease and flour a Bundt pan; set aside.
2. In a medium bowl, stir together both flours, sugar, cocoa, flax, baking soda, baking powder, salt, and cinnamon. Add the eggs, oil and applesauce; mix well. Fold in the walnuts and zucchini until they are evenly distributed. Pour into the prepared pan.
3. Bake for 50 to 60 minutes, until a toothpick inserted into the center comes out clean. Cool cake completely before adding your favourite frosting.

Cranberry Almond Coffee Cake – Makes one 9-inch cake

"This rich, intensely flavoured cake is perfect with a cup of coffee, and the cranberries make it deliciously seasonal"

2/3 cup packed dark brown sugar
1/3 cup butter
1.5 cups fresh cranberries, sliced in halves
1/2 cup sliced almonds

1/2 cup butter, room temperature
1/2 cup white sugar
1/4 cup dark brown sugar
2 large eggs
1 tablespoon instant coffee powder
1 teaspoon vanilla extract
1 cup sour cream
1/4 cup milk
1.5 cups flour
1.5 teaspoons baking powder
1 teaspoon baking soda
1 teaspoon ground cinnamon
1/4 teaspoon ground cloves
1/4 teaspoon ground nutmeg
1/2 teaspoon salt

1. Preheat oven to 350°F. Line a 9-inch springform pan with aluminum foil to prevent leaking, and then spray with baking spray.
2. In a small pot, combine the 2/3 cup brown sugar and the 1/3 cup butter. Bring to a boil over medium heat. Pour into the springform pan and sprinkle evenly with the cut cranberries and sliced almonds.
3. In a large mixing bowl or stand mixer, cream the 1/2 cup butter together with the 1/2 cup white sugar and 1/4 cup brown sugar until light and fluffy. Beat the eggs in one at a time. Stir in the instant coffee and vanilla.
4. In a small separate bowl, combine the sour cream and milk together and set aside.

5. In another small separate bowl, combine all the remaining dry ingredients and set aside.
6. To the egg/sugar mixture, gently mix in the flour mixture in 2 parts with the sour cream mixture in 1 part, until you form one batter.
7. Pour the batter into the prepared pan over the cranberries and almonds.
8. Bake for 1 hour or until an inserted toothpick comes out clean.
9. Cool in pan for 10 minutes before inverting onto a serving plate. Carefully remove the pan with the foil and serve.

Eggnog Bread Pudding – Makes 6 portions
Recipe Courtesy of Leanne Witherly, BC Egg

1 loaf of challah bread, or country-style white bread
3 large eggs
3/4 cup brown sugar
3 cups eggnog
1 cup whipping cream
1 teaspoon vanilla extract
2 tablespoons bourbon, optional
Pinch of salt
1/2 teaspoon freshly grated nutmeg

1. Cut bread into roughly 1" cubes. Day old bread is best for this as it holds up better once the liquid is added.
2. Grease a 9x13 pan and set aside. You can use a narrower and deeper pan if you prefer a pudding that is gooier with less "crunch" on top. Baking time may need to be adjusted.
3. Whisk together eggs and brown sugar till the sugar is dissolved. Add in eggnog, cream, vanilla, bourbon, salt, and nutmeg. Mix well.
4. Layer bread cubes in pan. Pour eggnog mixture evenly over the bread.
5. Cover and chill in the fridge for at least 2 hours or overnight.
6. When ready to bake uncover and give the bread a squish to ensure the top layers are moist and have absorbed the custard.
7. Bake for 50 to 60 minutes at 350°F until the custard is set.
8. Serve as is, or with whipped cream and additional ground nutmeg.

Eggnog Cheesecake – makes 16 portions
Recipe Courtesy of BC Egg, bcegg.com

1.5 cups graham cracker crumbs
1/4 cup melted butter
2 tablespoons white sugar
4 packages (8 oz/250 g) brick-style cream cheese, room temperature
1 cup white sugar
1.25 teaspoons freshly grated nutmeg
1/4 teaspoon salt
4 large eggs
2.5 teaspoons rum extract, or 2 tablespoons spiced rum or bourbon
1 cup whipping cream
2 tablespoons white sugar
1 teaspoon vanilla extract
Freshly grated nutmeg

1. Line inside of a 9-inch (23 cm) springform cake pan with parchment paper strip. Set pan on a large piece of heavy-duty foil (or double layer of regular foil) & wrap sides then place in deep roasting pan.
2. Preheat oven to 350°F. Toss the graham cracker crumbs with the melted butter and 2 tablespoons white sugar. Firmly press into the bottom of the springform pan. Bake until lightly golden, for 10 to 15 minutes. Cool completely.
3. Reduce heat to 325°F. Beat cream cheese until smooth. Beat in 1 cup sugar, 1.25 teaspoons nutmeg and salt until fluffy. Beat in eggs, one at a time. Beat in rum extract. Pour over crust.
4. Pour water into roasting pan halfway up sides of the springform pan.
5. Bake until set but jiggles slightly in centre, about 70 minutes. Turn off the oven and leave inside for 1 hour. Transfer to wire rack and cool in its water bath. Remove from water. Cool to room temperature. Chill overnight or up to 2 days. Remove spring form pan before serving.
6. When ready to serve, beat whipping cream with 2 tablespoons sugar and vanilla extract until stiff. Dollop whipped cream over top of cheesecake or onto individual servings. Grate nutmeg overtop.

NOTES: Use vanilla extract instead of the rum extract, if desired.

Cranberry Bread Pudding – Makes 10 to 12 portions

1 – 454g (1 pound) French loaf
4 large eggs, beaten
1.25 cups sugar
1 teaspoon vanilla extract
1 teaspoon ground cinnamon
1/4 teaspoon salt
Zest from 2 lemons, finely chopped
2 cups 10%MF cream (half and half)
2 cups milk
3/4 cup sweetened dried cranberries
3/4 cup cranberries (fresh or frozen), halved
Vanilla bean ice cream, optional

1. Preheat oven to 400°F. Tear the French bread into approximate 1-inch to 2-inch chunks and spread evenly on a large baking sheet. Bake in the oven for 10 minutes, tossing the pieces around about halfway through. Remove from the oven and let sit while you prepare the rest of the pudding.
2. Decrease the oven temperature to 350°F and prepare a 9x13-inch baking dish by buttering it.
3. In a large bowl, combine the eggs, sugar, vanilla, cinnamon, salt, and the zest thoroughly. Whisk in the cream and milk. Add the toasted bread pieces and the dried cranberries and toss together thoroughly with your hands. Let sit for 10 minutes for the bread pieces to absorb.
4. Put one half of the custard-soaked bread mixture into the prepared baking dish and top with half of the fresh/frozen halved cranberries. Add the remaining bread mixture (and scrape all liquid from the bowl) to the dish and top with the remaining fresh/frozen halved cranberries. Bake for approximately 45 minutes until the top browns and puffs up. Also, an inserted butter knife should come out clean.
5. Let sit for at least 10 to 15 minutes before serving warm with vanilla bean ice cream.

Lemon Glazed Pound Cake

"Originating in Europe in the first half of the 18th century, this traditional loaf weighed 4 pounds, because of creating it with one pound of each of its four ingredients. Break out your kitchen scale for this one."

Cake
1-pound (454g) butter, room temperature
1-pound (454g) white sugar
1-pound (454g) eggs (approximately 8 to 9 large eggs)
2 teaspoons vanilla extract
1-pound (454g) all-purpose flour
1 teaspoon salt

Glaze
1 cup icing sugar
Zest of 1 lemon, finely chopped/grated
Juice of 1 lemon
1/4 teaspoon salt

1. Preheat oven to 350°F. Prepare 2 standard loaf pans with baking spray or butter.
2. In a stand mixer, beat the butter and sugar together thoroughly on high speed until fluffy and pale, about 2 to 3 minutes, scraping down the bowl and paddle occasionally.
3. Put the eggs in a pourable container (like an extra-large measuring cup) along with the vanilla. Put the mixer on medium-low speed and pour in the eggs one at a time (estimate by one yolk at a time), gradually increase speed to medium until thoroughly combined, scraping down the bowl and paddle occasionally.
4. Mix the 1 teaspoon of salt into the flour. Gently fold in the flour mixture 1/2 at a time until just combined. Do not overmix.
5. Scoop batter evenly into the 2 prepared loaf pans and smooth the batter with a spatula.
6. Bake for approximately 50 to 60 minutes until an inserted toothpick comes out clean. Let cool in the pans for about 5 to 10 minutes, before removing from the pans and transferring to a cooling rack.

7. Once the cakes are room temperature, in a small bowl mix the icing sugar, zest, lemon juice, and 1/4 teaspoon of salt together and pour evenly over the loafs. Slice and serve.

Makes 2 loaf pans of cake

Maple Pecan Crunch Eggy Bread

Recipe Courtesy of BC Egg, bcegg.com

Bread

1 large loaf "rustique" or French country bread (1 1/2 loaves if medium sized)
8 large eggs
2 cups 2% or whole milk
1 cup 18% coffee cream
1/2 cup packed brown sugar
1/2 cup maple syrup, plus extra for garnish
1 teaspoon ground cinnamon
1 teaspoon ground ginger
1/4 teaspoon ground nutmeg
1/4 teaspoon ground allspice
1 teaspoon vanilla extract
Pinch of salt
1/4 cup melted butter
Zest of a clementine or 1/2 an orange
1 cup fresh blueberries

Topping

1/2 cup all-purpose flour
1/2 cup packed brown sugar
1/2 cup rolled oats
1 cup whole pecans
1/2 teaspoon ground cinnamon
Pinch of salt
1/2 cup melted butter

Garnish

Plain or vanilla Greek yogurt
Fresh blueberries
Maple syrup

1. Either tear or roughly cube the bread and place in a large mixing bowl. Do not cut off the crust, as it adds a nice texture to the eggy bread.
2. In a second bowl, place the eggs, milk, cream, brown sugar, 1/2 cup of maple syrup, spices, vanilla, salt, melted butter, and clementine or orange zest. Whisk until a smooth custard forms.
3. Pour the custard over the bread and add the fresh blueberries. Mix very well.
4. Prepare a large casserole or lasagna pan by greasing it with a little butter, canola oil, or food release spray. Fill the dish with the egg-soaked bread and wrap in plastic wrap. Refrigerate for several hours, preferably overnight.
5. When ready to bake, preheat your oven to 350°F with the rack in the center. Add the flour, brown sugar, oats, pecans, cinnamon, and salt for the topping in a bowl. Pour over the melted butter and toss very well. Spread the topping over the eggy bread in the casserole dish.
6. Bake for about 1 hour, checking the center of the dish for firmness after 45 minutes. It should feel firm in the center but not appear too dark on the edges. To serve, remove from the oven and allow to rest for 10 minutes. Add a generous dollop of Greek yogurt, a sprinkle of fresh blueberries, and a good pour of maple syrup before serving.

Makes 10 portions

Rum Raisin Bread Pudding

1/2 cup raisins
1/2 cup currants
1/2 packed cup pitted dates, chopped fine
1 cup boiling water
1 – 454g (1 pound) French loaf
Butter for the pan
4 large eggs, beaten
1 cup sugar
1 teaspoon vanilla extract
1 teaspoon ground cinnamon
1/2 teaspoon ground cloves
1/2 teaspoon ground nutmeg
1/2 teaspoon salt
Zest from 2 lemons, finely chopped
1 apple, cored & grated
2 cups 10%MF cream (half and half)
2 cups milk (2%MF or 3.5%Homogenized)
2 tablespoons butter
1 – 300ml can sweetened condensed milk
2 to 3 tablespoons dark rum
Vanilla bean ice cream
Mint leaves, optional

1. Preheat oven to 400°F.
2. Let the raisins, currants and dates soak in the boiling water for 20 minutes, then drain and set aside.
3. Tear the French bread into approximate 1-inch to 2-inch chunks and spread evenly on a large baking sheet. Bake in the oven for 10 minutes, tossing the pieces around about halfway through. Remove from the oven and set aside.
4. Decrease the oven temperature to 350°F and prepare a 9x13 baking dish by buttering it.
5. In a large bowl, combine the eggs, sugar, vanilla, cinnamon, cloves, nutmeg, salt, and the zest thoroughly. Stir in the grated apple and the

drained reserved raisins, currants and dates. Whisk in the cream and milk. Add the reserved toasted bread pieces and toss together thoroughly with your hands. Let sit for 10 minutes for the bread pieces to absorb.

6. Transfer this mixture evenly into the prepared baking dish (and scrape all liquid from the bowl). Dot the surface with small bits of the 2 tbsp butter. Bake for approximately 45 to 60 minutes until the top browns and puffs up. Also, an inserted butter knife should come out clean. Let sit for 10 to 15 minutes before cutting.

7. Empty the can of sweetened condensed milk into a pot and heat gently until warm. Remove from the heat and stir in the rum.

8. Plate the bread pudding pieces warm with vanilla bean ice cream, drizzled with rum sauce, and each garnished with a sprig of fresh mint.

Makes 12 portions

Sticky Toffee Pudding

"This is so rich, moist, and delicious that it may become a tradition in your family to make for special occasions or holidays"

Pudding
2/3 cup finely chopped dried pitted dates (not dates from a brick)
1/2 cup finely chopped pitted prunes
1 cup orange juice
2 teaspoons room temperature butter for the pan
1 cup all-purpose flour
3/4 teaspoon baking powder
3/4 teaspoon baking soda
1/2 teaspoon salt
1/4 teaspoon of EACH: cinnamon, cloves, nutmeg, allspice
1 cup butter, room temperature
1 cup dark brown sugar
2 large eggs
1 teaspoon vanilla extract

Sauce
3/4 cup butter
1 cup whipping cream
3/4 cup dark brown sugar
1/8 teaspoon salt
1/2 teaspoon vanilla extract
Up to 3 tablespoons dark rum, brandy, or whiskey, if desired

Garnish
Vanilla ice cream, for serving
Fresh mint leaves, for garnish, optional

1. Place the dates, prunes, and orange juice in a small pot. Bring to a boil over medium-high heat and cook until this mixture has become a thick paste, approximately 6 to 9 minutes, stirring frequently. Transfer this mixture to a stainless-steel bowl, or wide shallow dish, and cool slightly

in the fridge (to speed this process, you can put it in the freezer, but keep an eye on it as you don't want it frozen).

2. Preheat oven to 350°F and butter a 9-inch square pan with the 2 teaspoons butter.

3. Combine the flour, baking powder, baking soda, 1/2 teaspoon salt, 1/4 teaspoon ground cinnamon, 1/4 teaspoon ground cloves, 1/4 teaspoon ground nutmeg, and 1/4 teaspoon ground allspice in a mixing bowl. Set aside.

4. In a separate bowl, or stand mixer, cream the 1 cup butter and 1 cup brown sugar together until light and fluffy. Mix in the eggs one at a time, followed by the 1 teaspoon vanilla, combining well, and scraping down the bowl a few times during this process. Slowly stir in the reserved date/prune mixture. Gently incorporate the reserved flour mixture until a smooth batter is formed.

5. Pour the batter into the prepared pan and bake for approximately 30 to 35 minutes until dark and cooked through and the centre springs back when lightly pressed (you are looking for an internal temperature of 200°F to 205°F). Let stand at room temperature for at least 5 minutes before cutting into 9 equal squares.

6. While pudding is in the oven, make the sauce: In a medium pot over medium heat, melt the 3/4 cup butter. Stir in the whipping cream, 3/4 cup brown sugar, and 1/8 teaspoon salt. Bring to a low rolling boil and cook for approximately 10 minutes, stirring occasionally, until thickened and syrupy (adjusting the heat to medium-low as needed to prevent boiling over). Remove from the heat and stir in the vanilla and optional liquor. This should make approximately 2 cups of sauce.

7. Portion each piece of pudding into small dessert bowls. Serve the sauce equally over the portions (approximately 3 to 4 tablespoons each portion), top with vanilla ice cream, garnish each with fresh mint if desired, and serve immediately.

Makes 9 portions

COOKIES

Chocolate Marble Icebox Cookies

Recipe Courtesy of BC Egg, bcegg.com

1 cup butter, softened
1 cup white sugar
2 large eggs
2 teaspoons vanilla extract
3 cups all-purpose flour
1.5 teaspoons baking powder
1/2 teaspoon salt
2 ounces unsweetened chocolate, melted

1. In a large bowl beat butter with sugar until light and fluffy. Beat in eggs one at a time then add the vanilla. In a separate bowl whisk together the flour, baking powder and salt. Stir into the butter mixture in two additions until smooth.
2. Divide dough in half and pour the melted chocolate over one half and stir to combine. Add the plain dough back in and stir roughly to make a marbled effect.
3. Divide the dough into thirds and place each on a large square of parchment paper. Roll into a 13-inch log and wrap in parchment paper, twisting the ends to secure them. Refrigerate until firm – at least 3 hours (logs can be refrigerated for up to 3 days).
4. Cut logs into 1/3-inch-thick slices. Place 1 inch apart on pans. Bake in a 350F oven for 12 to 14 minutes. Let cool on pans for 5 minutes before transferring to a rack to cool completely. Baked cookies can be frozen for up to 2 weeks.

Cranberry White Chocolate Biscotti

Recipe Courtesy of BC Egg, bcegg.com

2 cups all-purpose flour
1.5 teaspoons baking powder
3/4 cup white sugar
1/2 cup butter, room temperature
1 teaspoon grated orange zest
1/4 teaspoon salt
2 large eggs
3/4 cup white chocolate chips
2/3 cup dried cranberries
12 ounces good-quality white chocolate, chopped
2/3 cup slivered almonds, optional

1. Preheat oven to 350°F and line a baking sheet with parchment paper.
2. In a medium bowl, whisk the flour and baking powder together.
3. Using an electric mixer, beat the sugar, butter, orange zest, and salt together in a large bowl. Beat in the eggs 1 at a time.
4. Add the flour mixture and beat just until combined. Stir in the white chocolate chips and dried cranberries.
5. Form the dough into two 12-inch long, 3-inch-wide logs on the prepared baking sheet. If the dough is very sticky, refrigerate for 10 minutes, or form logs right on the parchment or baking sheets. Rough shaping is fine.
6. Bake for about 40 minutes, until just golden. Cool for 30 minutes.
7. Place the log on a cutting board. Using a sharp serrated knife, cut the log on a diagonal into 1/2 to 3/4-inch-thick slices. Arrange the biscotti, cut side down, on the baking sheet.
8. Bake the biscotti a second time for about 15 minutes at 350°F, until they are pale golden. Transfer the biscotti to a rack and cool completely.
9. Gently melt the chopped white chocolate in a heatproof bowl set over a saucepan of simmering water, stirring, and scraping down the sides. Drizzle this white chocolate over the biscotti, or dip half of the biscotti into the melted chocolate. Gently shake off the excess chocolate. Place

the biscotti on the baking sheet for the chocolate to set. Refrigerate until the chocolate is firm, about 35 minutes.

10. The biscotti can be stored in an airtight container up to 4 days, or wrap them in foil and freeze in resealable plastic bags up to 3 weeks.

Gluten Free Chocolate Chip Cookies

Recipe Courtesy of Amanda Brittain, BC Egg

250g butter, room temperature
1 cup brown sugar
1 large egg
2 cups gluten-free baking cup-for-cup substitute such as Cloud 9
1.25 teaspoons baking powder
45g desiccated coconut
220g chocolate chips
185g toasted chopped nuts such as hazelnuts, walnuts, pecans

1. Preheat oven to 350°F.
2. Beat butter and sugar in a bowl until light and fluffy. Beat in egg.
3. Add sifted gluten-free baking substitute, baking powder, coconut, chocolate chips, and nuts to butter mixture and stir to combine.
4. Drop tablespoons of mixture onto baking trays lined with parchment paper and bake for 12 to 15 minutes or until cookies are golden. Transfer to a wire rack to cool.

Makes approximately 35 cookies

Eggnog Biscotti

Recipe Courtesy of Leanne Witherly, BC Egg

1/2 cup butter, room temperature
3/4 cup white sugar
2 large eggs
1/2 teaspoon vanilla extract
1 tablespoon spiced rum or bourbon
2.25 cups all-purpose flour
1.5 teaspoons baking powder
1/4 teaspoon salt
1 teaspoon fresh grated nutmeg, divided
6 ounces white chocolate

1. Preheat oven to 350°F and line 2 baking sheets with parchment paper.
2. Beat butter and sugar together in an electric mixer until light and fluffy.
3. Add eggs one at a time, mixing well until each egg is completely incorporated. Then add the vanilla and bourbon and beat until well combined.
4. In a separate bowl, combine the flour, baking powder, salt, and 1/2 teaspoon of the nutmeg. Slowly add this dry mixture to the eat ingredients until just blended.
5. Split the dough into 2 portions. With lightly floured hands, form each portion into a log on the prepared baking sheets, about 13 inches long and 3 inches wide.
6. Bake until golden, about 50 minutes, rotating the pans halfway through baking.
7. Cool at room temperature for 30 minutes.
8. Once cooled, placed logs on a cutting board and with a sharp serrated knife cut logs crosswise into 1/2-inch to 3/4-inch thick slices. Arrange the biscotti cut side down back on the baking sheets.
9. Bake biscotti for a second time for 10 minutes, flip, and bake for another 5 to 10 minutes until both sides are light golden brown. Transfer to a rack and cool completely.
10. For the white chocolate drizzle: Dice white chocolate into fine pieces and place in a glass bowl. Add a few inches of boiling water to a larger

bowl and set the bowl of chocolate inside, being careful not to let any water mix with the chocolate. Stir well as the heat from the water gently melts the chocolate. Mix in the remaining 1/2 teaspoon of nutmeg, then drizzle or dip the biscotti with chocolate.

11. Place the biscotti back on the parchment lined baking sheets for the chocolate to set, refrigerating if necessary.

Spiced Ginger Molasses Cookies
Recipe Courtesy of BC Egg, BCegg.com

3/4 cup butter, room temperature
1 cup sugar
1 large egg
1/4 cup molasses
2 cups all-purpose flour
1 teaspoon baking powder
1 teaspoon ground cinnamon
1 teaspoon ground cloves
1 teaspoon ground ginger
Sugar for rolling

1. Preheat oven to 325°F.
2. Cream together butter and sugar until fluffy. Add in egg and molasses and mix well.
3. Sift together flour, baking powder and spices. Gradually add dry ingredients to butter mixture until fully incorporated.
4. Shape dough into 1-inch balls and roll each ball in sugar.
5. Place the prepared dough balls 2 inches apart on a greased or parchment lined baking sheet. Bake for 12 to 15 minutes or until golden and the surface is cracked and crinkly.
6. Cool on sheets for at least 10 minutes before moving to wire racks to cool completely.

Gingerbread Cookies
Recipe Courtesy of BC Egg, bcegg.ca

Cookies
4 cups all-purpose flour
1 tablespoon ground ginger
2 teaspoons ground cinnamon
1/4 teaspoon ground cloves
1/4 teaspoon ground nutmeg
1.5 teaspoons baking powder
1/2 cup shortening
1/2 cup butter
1.75 cups brown sugar
1/3 cup molasses
2 large eggs

Butter Icing
1.5 cups icing sugar
3 tablespoons butter, room temperature
1 tablespoon vanilla extract
1 tablespoon milk
3 drops food colouring, optional

1. In a medium sized bowl, mix the flour, ginger, cinnamon, cloves, nutmeg, and baking powder together.
2. In a large bowl, place the shortening, butter, and brown sugar. Cream together with an electric mixer; add molasses and beat until blended.
3. Break the eggs into the sugar mixture and beat until eggs are completely blended in.
4. Add half the flour mixture in the butter mixture and stir to combine. Add remainder of the flour mixture and continue blending. Mixture will be thick.
5. Lightly flour a clean kitchen surface and roll out the dough to 1/4-inch thickness. Line cookie sheets with parchment paper.
6. Using cookie cutters, cut out gingerbread men and gingerbread ladies, and place on parchment paper and bake at 350°F for 12 to 13 minutes.

7. Butter Icing: Combine icing sugar, butter, vanilla, and milk, beating until creamy. Thin with a few more drops of milk (if necessary) to reach desired spreading consistency. Stir in optional food colouring or leave icing white. Spread frosting over cooled cookies. Decorate with your choice of candies and sprinkles.

Makes approximately 30 cookies, depending on size of cookie cutters`

RECIPE NOTES

Lemon Poppy Seed Cookies

"Using a 1-ounce cookie scoop (black handle) to portion out the dough works great"

Cookies

1/2 cup fresh lemon juice
1 cup butter, room temperature
1 cup white sugar
1 large egg
2 teaspoons vanilla extract
Finely grated zest of 1 lemon
2 cups all-purpose flour
1 teaspoon baking soda
1/2 teaspoon salt
1 tablespoon poppy seeds

Glaze

1.5 cups icing sugar
1 tablespoon poppy seeds
Finely grated zest of 1 lemon
2.5 tablespoons fresh lemon juice
1/4 teaspoon salt

1. Preheat oven to 375°F and line 2 baking sheets with parchment paper.
2. In a small stainless-steel pot, boil the 1/2 cup lemon juice over medium heat until reduced to 2 tablespoons. Transfer out of the pot into a small dish and set aside in the fridge to cool.
3. Using a handheld electric mixer, or a stand mixer with a paddle attachment, cream the butter and white sugar together on medium speed until fully combined and whipped, approximately 3 minutes. Scrape down the sides of the bowl. Add the egg, vanilla, lemon zest, and the 2 tablespoons reserved reduced lemon juice and beat until fully combined, approximately 1 minute.
4. In a separate mixing bowl combine the flour, baking soda, salt, and poppy seeds. Slowly add this dry mixture into the butter/sugar mixture, on a lower speed while gradually increasing speed to medium, to combine thoroughly without overmixing.

5. Place 1.5-inch dough balls approximately 3 inches apart on the prepared baking sheets.
6. Bake for approximately 15-17 minutes until the cookies have spread out and the edges have browned. (Internal temp should be 175°F – 185°F if you want to check)
7. Place the baking sheets on wire racks to cool the cookies to room temperature before glazing.
8. To make the glaze: in a small bowl mix the icing sugar, 1 tablespoon poppy seeds, lemon zest, 2.5 tablespoons lemon juice, and 1/4 teaspoon of salt together. Glaze the cookies when they are room temperature.

Makes approximately 20 cookies

Sugar Cookies
Recipe Courtesy of BC Egg, BCegg.com

Cookies
1 cup white sugar
1 cup butter
1 teaspoon vanilla extract
2 large eggs
2.5 cups all-purpose flour
2 teaspoons baking powder
1/2 teaspoon salt

Glaze Icing
1.5 cups icing sugar
3 tablespoons milk
1/8 teaspoon almond extract
3 drops food colouring, optional

1. With an electric mixture, beat sugar, butter and vanilla until mixture is creamy, about 2 minutes. Scrape down sides of bowl. Add eggs, beating after each egg; beat thoroughly.
2. In a separate bowl combine flour, baking powder and salt. Beat the dry ingredients into the creamed mixture.
3. Roll out cookie dough to 1/4-inch thick onto a lightly floured board. For best results, do not roll cookie dough too thin. Use cookie cutters of your choice for a variety of different shapes and sizes. Place cookies on parchment lined cookie sheets.
4. Bake at 350°F for 10 minutes or until the underside of cookies turn golden brown.
5. For the glaze icing, combine icing sugar with milk to reach desired spreading consistency. Stir in food colouring or leave icing white. Using a pastry brush, paint frosting over cooled cookies and decorate with coloured sugar, toasted coconut or slivered almonds, chocolate shavings or chocolate chips.

Makes approximately 4 dozen cookies

RECIPE NOTES

DESSERTS

Perfect Pie Pastry

Recipe Courtesy of Mrs. Chef Dez (Katherine Desormeaux)

"I like to cut in the shortening and grate the butter for the optimum texture and flavour. This is the combination I prefer, but you can feel free to play around with the ratio of butter to shortening as long as you use a total of 2 1/4 cups of fat. Shortening contributes to a lighter pastry and butter makes a more flavourful pastry."

5 cups flour
3 teaspoons brown sugar
1 teaspoon salt
1 teaspoon baking powder
1 pound shortening very cold
1/4 cup frozen butter
1 large egg
1 tablespoon white vinegar
Cold water

1. Combine flour, sugar, salt and baking powder.
2. Cut in shortening with a pastry cutter then, using a medium sized grater, grate the butter in and stir to distribute.
3. In a liquid measuring cup, lightly beat egg and vinegar and add enough water to fill to 3/4 cup measure. Stir into the flour mixture just until moistened and divide the dough into four equal portions.
4. Shape each into a flat disk and wrap in plastic wrap. Refrigerate for at least 1/2 hour, and then roll out.

This recipe makes enough pastry for two double-crust pies, or 4 single-crust pies and it freezes well.

Amaretto Truffles with Vanilla Pastry Cream

"This chocolate dessert is well worth the effort of getting your hands a bit dirty"

Truffles

1 cup semi-sweet chocolate chips
1/4 cup butter
2 tablespoons icing sugar, sifted
2 tablespoons cream cheese, room temperature
3 tablespoons amaretto
Unsweetened cocoa powder
Sliced almonds, crushed

1. In a double boiler, gently melt the chocolate and the butter together until smooth and fully combined.
2. Remove from the heat and stir in the icing sugar, then the cream cheese until fully combined and lump free.
3. Stir in the amaretto and chill in the refrigerator until solid (min. 2 hours).
4. Using a spoon, quickly scoop out a heaping teaspoon of the mixture, roll and press it into a ball in your hands, and then roll it in cocoa powder or almonds. Do each one individually and set aside before moving on to the next one, to help prevent melting of the chocolate.

Vanilla Pastry Cream

1 cup milk
1/4 cup white sugar
1 teaspoon vanilla extract
1/8 teaspoon salt
3 egg yolks
1 tablespoon flour, sifted
1.5 teaspoons cornstarch, sifted
More amaretto and fresh mint leaves for garnish

1. In a heavy bottomed pot, mix the milk, sugar, vanilla, and salt together and bring to a boil over medium-high heat, stirring frequently.

2. Beat the egg yolks with the flour and cornstarch until it becomes pale yellow.
3. Starting very slowly, gradually add the hot milk to the beaten yolks to ensure that the eggs don't get too hot all at once.
4. Return the mixture to the pot and bring to a boil over medium heat while whisking constantly, approximately 2 to 3 minutes. It is at the boiling point that the mixture will thicken. Spoon into a separate bowl and chill.

For each portion, place a dollop of pastry cream in a martini glass, and nestle 3 truffles in the pastry cream. Drizzle with a teaspoon of amaretto and garnish with a fresh mint leaf.

Makes Approximately 12 – 15 truffles (4 to 5 servings)

Classic Vanilla Cupcakes

Recipe Courtesy of BC Egg, bcegg.com

Cupcakes

1.5 cups all-purpose flour, sifted
1.5 teaspoons baking powder
1/2 teaspoon salt
1/2 cup butter, room temperature
1 cup white sugar
2 large eggs, room temperature
2 teaspoons vanilla extract
3/4 cup milk

Frosting

1/2 cup butter, room temperature
4 cups icing sugar, sifted
1/4 cup whipping cream (approx.)
2 teaspoons vanilla extract
Pinch salt

1. Preheat oven to 350°F. Line 12 muffin cups with paper liners. Whisk together flour, baking powder and salt; set aside. In separate bowl and using electric mixer, beat 1/2 cup butter with the white sugar until light and fluffy. Beat in eggs, one at a time, incorporating each one fully before adding the next one; beat in 2 teaspoons vanilla.
2. With mixer on low speed, add the reserved flour mixture in 3 parts alternately with the milk in 2 parts, starting and ending with flour mixture, and scraping bowl as needed between additions.
3. Spoon or scoop batter into prepared muffin cups, about two-thirds full. Bake for 18 to 20 minutes or until tester comes out clean when inserted into center of cupcakes. Let cool completely on rack.
4. Prepare the frosting: Beat 1/2 cup butter until light and fluffy. With mixer on low speed, beat in icing sugar, whipping cream, 2 teaspoons vanilla and a pinch of salt until smooth, adding up to 2 tbsp more whipping cream if needed. Increase speed to high and beat for 1 to 2 minutes or until frosting is light and fluffy.

5. Add frosting to piping bag fitted with round tip and pipe over cupcakes. Alternatively, spoon frosting into resealable bag and clip off one corner to pipe over cupcakes, or spoon onto cupcakes.

Makes 12 portions

Crème Brulée – Makes 4 portions
"A delicious classic dessert that has only 5 ingredients"

2.25 cups whipping cream
6 egg yolks
6 tablespoons white sugar
1/4 teaspoon salt
1.5 teaspoons vanilla extract
4 to 6 teaspoons white sugar, for caramelizing

1. Preheat oven to 325°F. Place four 1 cup ramekins or custard cups in a baking dish. Set aside.
2. Heat cream in saucepan over medium-high heat until small bubbles form around edge of pan. Meanwhile, whisk egg yolks, 6 tablespoons of sugar, and the salt until thick and pale lemon-coloured – about 1 to 2 minutes.
3. When cream is hot, gradually whisk into egg yolk mixture. Stir in vanilla. Pour mixture through sieve into ramekins, dividing evenly. Pour very hot water into baking dish to reach halfway up ramekins. Carefully place baking dish in oven. Bake until mostly set but with a slight jiggle in the centre, about 55 to 60 minutes.
4. Carefully remove ramekins from water. Cool on wire rack. When cool, cover with plastic wrap and refrigerate for least 2 hours or up to 2 days.
5. Just before serving (or up to 2 hours before serving), sprinkle sugar evenly over surface of desserts (1 to 1.5 teaspoons each). Using a mini torch or by placing the ramekins directly under the broiler, heat until sugar melts and caramelizes. Serve immediately, or for a firmer texture, chill until serving time.

Crème Caramel – Makes 6 portions

Butter for the ramekins
2/3 cup sugar
1/3 cup water
1/4 teaspoon salt
2 cups whipping cream
1 cup milk
1 teaspoon vanilla extract or vanilla bean paste
1/2 teaspoon salt
One 2-inch strip of lemon zest
3 large eggs
3 large egg yolks
1/2 cup sugar

1. Preheat oven to 350°F and grease 6 ramekins with butter.
2. Put the 2/3 cup sugar, 1/3 cup water and 1/4 tsp salt in a small heavy bottomed saucepan over medium/low heat until the sugar dissolves. When it starts to turn brown, swirl in the pan but do not stir until it turns dark rich brown, but not burnt. Immediately pour equal amounts into the prepared ramekins.
3. In another heavy bottomed saucepan, bring the whipping cream, milk, vanilla, salt and the lemon zest to just below a simmer over medium heat. Turn off the heat and let sit while preparing the eggs in the next step.
4. Whisk the 3 whole eggs with the 3 extra egg yolks and the 1/2 cup sugar until frothy.
5. Remove the zest from the cream mixture. Very slowly drizzle the hot cream mixture into the egg mixture while whisking constantly. Doing it slow will prevent the eggs from curdling.
6. Pour this prepared custard mixture into the caramel lined ramekins.
7. Place the filled ramekins into a large pan. Pour boiling water into the pan until the water level reaches approximately half-way up the outer sides of the ramekins.

8. Carefully put this pan into the oven and reduce the temperature to 325°F. Bake for approximately 40 minutes or until the centers of the custards are almost set (cooked).
9. Refrigerate for a minimum of 2 hours and up to 2 days.
10. To Serve: Loosen custard in each ramekin by running a butter knife all around the edge of the custard. Invert a plate over the ramekin. Quickly flip ramekin/plate over & gently jiggle the custard/caramel come loose. Remove the ramekin & serve on the plate.

Lemon Soufflés – Makes 5 to 6 portions
"If you love the flavour of lemon, you will love this dessert"

Butter for the dishes
2 tablespoons butter
1.25 cups white sugar
7 tablespoons all-purpose flour
1/2 teaspoon baking powder
1/4 teaspoon salt
4 large eggs, whites and yolks separated
2 teaspoons grated lemon zest
1/2 cup fresh lemon juice
1 cup milk

1. Preheat oven to 300°F. Butter a 5 to 6 small ramekins. Place them in a large pan that will allow them to be baked bain-marie style (surrounded by boiling water).
2. In a med-large mixing bowl, cream the 2 tablespoons butter with the 3/4 cup of the sugar. Stir in the flour, baking powder, and salt.
3. In a separate bowl beat the egg whites to moist peaks, and then whip in the remaining 1/2 cup sugar until just mixed.
4. Beat the egg yolks. Add the egg yolks, zest, lemon juice, and milk to the dry ingredients. Fold in the whipped egg whites. Immediately pour into dishes.
5. Add boiling water to the bain-marie and bake for 55 to 60 minutes until golden brown and set. Let cool slightly on rack and then serve warm or room temperature.

Mocha Rum Chocolate Soufflés

"Soufflés are not as difficult as some people think, and this makes a wonderful dessert. Baking time will depend on the temperature of your raw eggs. The finished soufflés will deflate a bit as they sit, but this is normal."

Butter for ramekins
5 ounces (142g) semi-sweet baking chocolate
2 tablespoons dark rum
1 tablespoon instant coffee powder
1/4 teaspoon salt
6 tablespoons sugar, plus more for dusting ramekins
6 large eggs, yolks separated from whites
Fresh raspberries (or thawed from frozen), for serving
Whipped cream, for serving

1. Preheat oven to 375°F.
2. Prepare four 1-cup sized (250ml) oven safe ramekins by buttering them and then dusting them with sugar thoroughly, tapping out any excess sugar.
3. Chop the chocolate into small bits. Alternatively, instead of chopping, you can use 5 ounces of pure semi-sweet chocolate chips instead of the squares of baking chocolate.
4. Place a medium pot half filled with water on the stove and maintain a low simmer.
5. In a stainless-steel bowl (that is big enough to sit on the pot without touching the water), place the prepared chocolate, rum, instant coffee, salt, and 3 tablespoons of the sugar. Let this mixture slowly melt together by sitting over the simmering water until just melted (do not heat longer than necessary) and then stir to combine. Remove the bowl from the heat and stir in the egg yolks, one at a time, to this chocolate mixture.
6. Beat the egg whites in a stand mixture with whisk attachment until foamy, then add the remaining 3 tablespoons of sugar. With the sugar added, beat the egg whites on high speed until stiff peaks form. Stir approximately 1/3 of these whipped egg whites into the chocolate mixture. Gently fold in the remaining egg whites thoroughly.

7. Pour the soufflé mixture equally into the prepared ramekins. Once filled, tap them on the counter a few times to knock out any air bubbles. Place the filled ramekins on a baking sheet and bake in the oven for approximately 17 to 20 minutes (depending on the temperature of your eggs), until puffed up, set, and cracked on top.
8. Put each hot ramekin on a serving plate and top with the raspberries, dollops of whipped cream and serve immediately. Alternatively, you can serve at room temperature and then garnish, just keep in mind that the soufflés will deflate a bit as they sit but they are still excellent.

Makes 4 portions

Coconut Lime Mousse – Makes 6 portions

Recipe Courtesy of Sean Bromilow, diversivore.com

"A bright, airy, & delicious dessert that just happens to be pretty wildly healthy. At under 250 calories per serving, it's healthy enough to eat for breakfast."

1 cup coconut cream - see note
1/2 cup coconut milk
4 large eggs, separated
90g white sugar (a little under 1/2 cup)
1/2 cup lime juice
1 tablespoon finely chopped/grated lime zest
1/8 teaspoon salt
7 g gelatin (e.g. 1 packet Knox brand) - see note
1/4 cup hot water

High-Speed Blender Version (Easier)

1. Place the coconut cream and coconut milk in a high-speed blender (e.g. Vitamix) along with the egg yolks, sugar, lime juice, and lime zest. Start the blender at the lowest speed and gradually increase it until it's running at the highest setting. Run the blender at high speed for 4 minutes before turning it off and allowing the mixture to cool until substantially (it should be near room temperature or lower before stirring in the egg whites).
2. In a separate large, non-reactive bowl, combine egg whites with a pinch of salt and whisk to stiff peaks.
3. Gently fold the whipped egg whites into the coconut/egg/lime mixture until just combined.
4. Dissolve gelatin in 1/4 cup of hot water, then gently whisk this into the coconut/egg/lime mixture. Stir until the gelatin is well mixes in but take care not to over-stir and deflate the whipped egg whites.
5. Pour the mousse into individual bowls or glasses and chill for at least 2 hours. Garnish with toasted coconut, yogurt (vanilla is good), fresh fruit, etc. For added texture and depth, serve with a good quality granola.

Traditional (No Blender) Version

1. Heat the coconut cream and coconut milk in a small saucepan over medium heat on the stove top. Stir regularly, keeping the heat low enough to keep the liquid very warm, but not boiling or simmering.
2. Whisk the egg yolks and sugar together in a small bowl until well-combined and glossy.
3. Temper the egg yolk mixture by slowly pouring about 1/2 cup of hot coconut cream into it while whisking briskly.
4. Pour tempered egg yolks into the rest of the coconut cream while whisking vigorously. Return the mixture to the stovetop and heat over a low flame, stirring regularly, until the mixture thickens enough to easily coat the back of a spoon. Remove from heat and refrigerate.
5. In a large bowl, combine the cooled coconut cream and egg mixture with the lime juice and zest. Whip until fairly well set and forming small peaks.
6. In a separate large, non-reactive bowl, combine egg whites with a pinch of salt and whisk to stiff peaks.
7. Gently fold the whipped egg whites into the coconut cream until the entire mixture is just combined.
8. Dissolve gelatin in 1/4 cup of hot water, then gently whisk this into the coconut mousse. Stir until the gelatin is well mixed in, but take care not to over-stir and deflate the whipped egg whites.
9. Pour the mousse into individual bowls or glasses and chill for at least 2 hours. Garnish with toasted coconut or fresh fruit. For added texture and depth, serve with a good quality granola.

NOTES

Coconut cream: coconut cream and coconut milk are not the same thing (and coconut water has nothing to do with this whatsoever). Much like dairy milk/cream, coconut milk (canned or homemade) will separate out into thicker cream on the top and thinner milk on the bottom. This recipe calls for 1 cup of the thicker cream layer and 1/2 cup of the thinner milk. If you've got well-mixed coconut milk, let it stand in the refrigerator for a few hours then scrape off the top cream layer.

Creamy Lime Custard Pie

Recipe Courtesy of Katherine Desormeaux (Mrs. Chef Dez)

"The optional food colouring enhances the presentation of the pie with a bright green lime appeal"

Crust
1/4 recipe of Perfect Pie Pastry (from this chapter)

Pie Filling
1 cup sugar
6 tablespoons cornstarch
1/4 teaspoon salt
2 cups milk
3 egg yolks, beaten
1/4 cup butter
1/2 cup cream cheese, softened in microwave
1/2 cup freshly squeezed lime juice
2 teaspoons finely chopped lime zest
2 - 3 drops green food colouring, optional

Meringue Topping
3 egg whites
pinch of cream of tartar
1/4 cup icing sugar

1. Roll out the pie crust and line a 9-inch pie plate. Trim the excess off the edge. Flute the edge for presentation. With a fork, poke holes in the bottom and sides of the crust to prevent air bubbles from forming. Blind bake the crust at 450°F for 12 to 15 minutes. Let cool at room temperature.
2. In a saucepan, combine the sugar, cornstarch, and salt. Slowly whisk in 1/4 cup of the milk. When smooth, whisk in the remainder of the milk. Turn the heat to medium-high and stir constantly until mixture is thick and bubbling. Remove from heat.
3. Slowly whisk 1 cup of the hot milk mixture into the beaten egg yolks, and then pour this yolk mixture back into the hot milk mixture in the

saucepan. Cook and whisk over medium heat for approximately 2 minutes until mixture is very thick and smooth.

4. Remove from the heat and stir in the butter. When the butter is melted, whisk in the softened cream cheese until there are no lumps. Stir in the lime juice, zest, and food colouring. Pour hot filling into baked pie crust.

5. Beat the egg whites and cream of tartar to soft peaks. Gradually add the icing sugar, beating until mixture forms medium/firm peaks. Immediately spread over the pie filling, ensuring to seal the meringue to the edges of the pie crust to prevent shrinkage.

6. Bake the pie at 350°F for 12 to 15 minutes or until meringue is golden brown.

7. Cool the pie to room temperature and refrigerate for at least 8 hours before serving.

8. Garnish with lime zest and twisted lime slices.

Guinness Brownies

"These are dark, rich, beautiful brownies with just a slight aftertaste of sweet bitterness from the Guinness. You will love these even if you don't like drinking Guinness."

Butter for the pan
1 – 440ml can Guinness beer, room temperature
4 large eggs
1 cup berry (superfine) sugar
3 cups pure semi-sweet chocolate chips (500g bag)
1/2 cup butter
1 cup flour
1 cup cocoa
Ice cream, whipped cream, or icing sugar for serving, optional

1. Preheat oven to 350°F. Butter a 9x13-inch pan.
2. Slowly pour the Guinness into a measuring cup or bowl to let the foam subside.
3. In a large bowl, beat the eggs and sugar together until light and fluffy.
4. In a double boiler, melt the chocolate chips with the butter, stirring until smooth. Remove from heat and add gradually while beating into the egg mixture.
5. Sift the flour and cocoa together.
6. To the chocolate/egg mixture, add the flour/cocoa mixture in three parts alternating with the Guinness in two parts, until well combined. The batter will seem very liquid.
7. Pour into the prepared pan and bake for approximately 30 minutes, or until an inserted toothpick in the centre comes out clean. Remove from the oven and let cool on a wire rack.
8. Cut into a maximum of 24 squares. Serve with ice cream, whip cream, or dust with icing sugar.

Lemon Zabaglione

"Also known as zabaione or sabayon, this is a light and frothy egg yolk dessert that is traditionally made with marsala wine. I prefer this lemon version over the classic preparation."

4 large egg yolks
1/4 cup white sugar
Pinch of salt
1/4 cup limoncello liqueur
1 tablespoon fresh lemon juice
Fresh berries for serving, optional

1. Bring 2 or 3 inches of water to a boil in a medium sized pot.
2. Place the egg yolks in a medium sized stainless steel mixing bowl along with the sugar and a pinch of salt. Whisk vigorously for 2 to 3 minutes until the mixture is thick and pale yellow in colour. Then vigorously whisk in the lemon liqueur and the lemon juice until thoroughly combined.
3. Reduce the heat to bring the water to a simmer and place the bowl on top of this pot while making sure that the bowl does not touch the water (we want the steam to gently and slowly cook this mixture). Whisk constantly over this simmering water until the mixture reaches a temperature of 145°F to 150°F and it turns very thick and frothy.
4. Remove from the heat and spoon into small dessert dishes and serve warm or cool slightly to room temperature and serve with the optional fresh berries.

Makes 4 small portions (approximately 1.25 cups for the total finished mixture)

Nanaimo Bars

Recipe Courtesy of Leanne Witherly, BC Egg

"Originating in (you guessed it!) Nanaimo, BC these tasty bars take a bit of work to prepare but are absolutely worth the effort! Our version has been handed down through three generations and definitely stand the test of time."

Base

1/2 cup butter, room temperature
5 tablespoons white sugar
5 tablespoons cocoa
1 large egg, beaten
1/2 teaspoon vanilla extract
1/2 cup chopped walnuts
1 cup shredded coconut
2 cups graham wafer crumbs

Icing

6 tablespoons butter, divided
2 tablespoons milk
2 tablespoons Bird's brand custard powder
2 cups icing sugar (powdered sugar)
4 squares semi-sweet baking chocolate

1. Add the 1/2 cup butter, 5 tablespoons white sugar, 5 tablespoons cocoa, and beaten egg to a non-stick pan and mix. Heat over medium-low heat until smooth and the consistency of custard. And the vanilla extract and stir well.
2. Remove from the heat and stir in the walnuts, coconut, and wafer crumbs. Press firmly into a 9 x 9 inch pan and cool completely.
3. Cream 4 tablespoons of the butter, milk, and custard powder together with an electric mixer. Slowly mix in the icing sugar and cream together. Spread this mixture over the chilled base and allow to harden (refrigerate as needed).
4. When the icing layer is set, melt the 4 squares of chocolate with the remaining 2 tablespoons of butter. Whisk until smooth. Spread this chocolate mixture over the icing layer and allow to harden.
5. Cut into squares or bars and enjoy!

Pumpkin Chiffon Pie

Recipe Courtesy of Katherine Desormeaux (Mrs. Chef Dez)

"Beating the egg whites separately and folding them in makes for a light chiffon texture. A warm spicy twist on a classic family favorite"

3/4 cup dark brown sugar, lightly packed
398ml can of pumpkin puree
1/4 teaspoon salt
1/2 teaspoon ground cinnamon
1/4 teaspoon ground nutmeg
1/4 teaspoon ground ginger
1/4 teaspoon ground cloves
1.25 cups milk
2 large eggs, separated
1 unbaked 9-inch pie crust

1. Lower oven rack to one level below center of oven. Preheat oven to 400°F.
2. In a large bowl, mix the brown sugar, pumpkin, salt, cinnamon, nutmeg, ginger, and cloves together in a large bowl.
3. Stir in milk. Beat the egg yolks and mix them in as well.
4. Beat egg whites to soft peaks and fold into the pumpkin mixture.
5. Pour into unbaked pie shell in a standard 9-inch pie plate.
6. Bake for 1 hour, rotating halfway through baking time.

Makes one 9-inch pie

MUFFINS, LOAVES, & BREADS

Banana Nut Muffins

Recipe Courtesy of Katherine Desormeaux (Mrs. Chef Dez), chefdez.com

2 cups whole wheat flour
1 cup brown sugar
1 teaspoon baking soda
1 teaspoon ground cinnamon
1/2 teaspoon ground nutmeg
1/2 teaspoon ground cloves
1 teaspoon salt
1/2 cup chopped nuts
2 large eggs, beaten
2.5 cups mashed bananas
1/2 cup canola oil
1 teaspoon grated lemon zest
1 teaspoon vanilla extract

1. Preheat oven to 350°F and prepare an 18-cup muffin tin with baking spray.
2. Combine the flour, sugar, baking soda, cinnamon, nutmeg, cloves, and salt together in a bowl. Toss in the chopped nuts of your choice.
3. In a separate bowl combine the eggs, bananas, oil, lemon zest, and vanilla together.
4. Add the wet ingredients to the dry ingredients and mix until just combined. DO NOT OVERMIX.
5. Divide batter equally into the 18 muffins cups and bake for approximately 20 -25 minutes. Cool 5 minutes in the pan before removing to a wire rack to cool completely.

Makes 18 muffins

Blueberry Bran Muffins

Recipe Courtesy of Katherine Desormeaux (Mrs. Chef Dez)

"Tossing the blueberries in the mixture of dry ingredients will help keep them suspended in the batter instead of sinking to the bottom"

1 cup whole wheat flour
1 cup natural bran
1 teaspoon baking powder
1 teaspoon baking soda
1/2 teaspoon salt
1 cup blueberries
1 large egg, beaten
1/3 cup canola oil
1/4 cup brown sugar
3 tablespoons maple syrup
1 teaspoon vanilla extract
1 cup buttermilk or sour milk *see notes below

1. Preheat oven to 375°F and prepare a 12-cup muffin tin with baking spray.
2. Combine the flour, bran, baking powder, baking soda, and salt together in a bowl. Toss in the blueberries.
3. In a separate bowl combine the egg, oil, sugar, syrup, vanilla, and buttermilk together.
4. Add the wet ingredients to the dry ingredients and mix until just combined. DO NOT OVERMIX.
5. Divide batter equally into the 12 muffins cups and bake for approximately 20 -25 minutes. Cool 5 minutes in the pan before removing to a wire rack to cool completely.

Makes 12 muffins

NOTES: Sour milk can be easily made by putting one teaspoon of lemon juice or vinegar into a one cup measure. Fill cup with milk and let sit for two minutes.

Brioche – Makes 12 portions
Recipe Courtesy of BC Egg, bcegg.com

1/2 cup homogenized milk, warmed
1/4 cup white sugar, divided
1 package (2.25 teaspoons) active dry yeast
4 large eggs, at room temperature
4 cups all-purpose flour, divided
1.5 teaspoons salt
3/4 cup unsalted butter, room temperature, cut into 12 cubes
1 large egg
1 tablespoon milk

1. In bowl of stand mixer, combine the 1/2 cup warmed milk, 1 teaspoon of the sugar, and the yeast; let stand 8 to 10 minutes or until foamy.
2. On low speed, beat in the 4 eggs, 1 cup of the flour, the remaining sugar, and salt until combined. Add the remaining flour; beat on low speed for 8 to 10 minutes or until the dough comes away cleanly from side of the bowl.
3. Beat in 1 cube of butter at a time, making sure each cube is incorporated before adding the next one; beat dough for about 5 minutes or satiny and glossy.
4. Transfer to greased bowl; cover with plastic wrap & let rise at room temperature 1.5 hours. Refrigerate at least 4 hours or up to 24 hours.
5. Let stand at room temperature for 2 to 2.5 hours or until doubled in volume. Divide dough into 8 portions and roll into balls. Divide balls evenly between 2 greased 8 x 4-inch (1.5 L) loaf pans. Cover with lightly greased plastic wrap; let stand at room temperature until doubled in volume.
6. Preheat oven to 375°F. Beat 1 egg with 1 tablespoon milk; brush evenly over loaves.
7. Bake for 40 to 45 minutes or until golden brown and instant-read thermometer registers 190°F (90°C) when inserted in centre of dough. If loaves brown too quickly, tent with foil.
8. Let cool in pans on rack for 10 minutes.
9. Remove from pans; let cool completely.

Carrot Bran Muffins

1.5 cups whole wheat flour
1.5 cups natural bran (aka wheat bran)
2/3 cup brown sugar
1/4 cup ground flax seed
2 teaspoons baking soda
1.5 teaspoons ground cinnamon
1/2 teaspoon salt
1/4 teaspoon ground cloves
1/4 teaspoon ground nutmeg
1 cup finely grated carrot
2 large eggs
1.5 cups milk
1/4 cup unsweetened apple sauce
1/4 cup canola oil
2 tablespoons lemon juice

1. Preheat oven to 400°F and prepare a 12-cup muffin pan with baking spray.
2. Combine the whole wheat flour, natural bran, brown sugar, ground flax seed, baking soda, cinnamon, salt, cloves, and nutmeg in a mixing bowl.
3. Toss the grated carrot into this dry mixture.
4. Beat the eggs thoroughly in a separate bowl.
5. Add the milk, apple sauce, canola oil, and lemon juice to the beaten eggs. Continue beating until thoroughly combined.
6. Combine the mixtures in the two bowls together until just mixed. Do not over mix.
7. Spoon the batter equally into the prepared muffin pan.
8. Bake for 20 minutes.
9. Cool slightly in the pan before serving.

Makes 12 large muffins

Cranberry Pistachio Banana Bread

"The half slice of banana on the top of the loaf gives this loaf a unique recognizable presentation"

1/2 cup butter, room temperature
1 cup sugar
1/2 cup dark brown sugar
4 large eggs
2 cups mashed very ripe bananas (approximately 4-6)
3 cups flour
4 teaspoons baking powder
1 teaspoon baking soda
1 teaspoon ground cinnamon
1/2 teaspoon salt
2 cups cranberries, roughly chopped, thawed if frozen
1.5 cups shelled salted pistachio nuts, left whole
1 yellow banana, sliced in half lengthwise

1. Preheat the oven to 350°F and prepare two standard bread loaf pans by spraying with baking spray.
2. Beat the butter and both sugars together with an electric mixer until thoroughly combined, approximately 2 minutes. Turn the speed to med-low and add 1 egg at a time until all 4 eggs are completely blended in. Stir in the mashed bananas.
3. In a large separate bowl add the flour, baking powder, baking soda, cinnamon, salt, and stir to combine. Add the cranberries and pistachios to this dry mixture to coat them with flour.
4. Add the wet egg/sugar/banana mixture to the dry ingredients and fold together until just combined – do not overmix.
5. Divide the batter between the two loaf pans and smooth out until even.
6. Place half of the yellow banana (cut side down) on the batter in each of the pans and bake for approximately 55 to 65 minutes, or until a toothpick inserted comes out clean.

Makes 2 loaves

Peppered Cheese Bread

"A quick bread with tons of cheese and pepper flavours! For best results make sure you use old (aged) cheddar and fresh cracked black pepper."

2 cups flour (plus more for dusting)
2 tablespoons sugar
4 teaspoons baking powder
1.5 teaspoons salt
1.5 teaspoons freshly cracked pepper
1 tablespoon soft green Madagascar peppercorns, drained - *optional
2 cups grated old cheddar cheese, divided
2 large eggs, beaten
1 cup milk
1 tablespoon melted butter
More pepper for sprinkling

1. Preheat oven to 350°F and prepare a 9-inch pie plate with baking spray and then dusting it with flour.
2. In a large bowl combine the 2 cups flour, sugar, baking powder, salt, and pepper. Toss in the green peppercorns (if using them) and 1.5 cups of the grated cheese to thoroughly coat with the flour mixture.
3. In a separate bowl mix together the eggs, milk, and melted butter.
4. Pour the wet mixture into the dry mixture. Stir until just combined and spread the mixture into the prepared pie plate.
5. Top with remaining 1/2 cup cheddar and more freshly cracked pepper.
6. Bake for approximately 30 to 35 minutes until the bread is solid and the cheese has browned slightly on top.
7. Let cool in the pie plate for at least 10 minutes before trying to remove it, and then let cool thoroughly on a cooling rack.

Makes one 9-inch round loaf

NOTES: Madagascar Green Peppercorns are soft peppercorns that come in a can and are sometimes hard to find. Specialty food stores usually have them, but you should call around first. If you can find them, I highly recommend using them in this recipe!

Popovers

Recipe Courtesy of Katherine Desormeaux (Mrs. Chef Dez)

"These are a favourite with our family – either as a side with dinner, or for breakfast with butter and honey. For the flour use either all-purpose flour, or 50% all-purpose and 50% whole wheat – using all whole wheat flour will make them too heavy."

2 tablespoons butter
4 large eggs, beaten
1.5 cups milk
1.5 cups flour
1 teaspoon salt

1. Preheat oven to 375°F and grease the cups of a 12-cup muffin tin heavily with the 2 tbsp butter.
2. Whisk the eggs and milk together. Add the flour & salt and continue whisking until combined (some lumps are fine).
3. Divide the mixture evenly into the muffin cups and bake for 25 to 30 minutes until golden brown. DO NOT OPEN THE OVEN DURING THE BAKING PROCESS OR THE POPOVERS WILL DEFLATE.
4. After removing them from the oven, pierce each popover with a fork to allow the steam to escape.

VARIATIONS

Try adding crushed garlic to the batter and sprinkling tops with parmesan cheese, or rosemary to the batter and cheddar cheese on top.

Makes 12 portions

Spiced Apple Loaf

Recipe Courtesy of Katherine Desormeaux (Mrs. Chef Dez)

"Use 1 cup whole wheat flour and 1 cup all-purpose, or 2 cups all-purpose – but using 2 cups whole wheat flour will make the loaf too heavy"

1 cup whole wheat flour
1 cup all-purpose flour
1.5 teaspoons ground cinnamon
1 teaspoon baking powder
1/2 teaspoon baking soda
1/2 teaspoon salt
1/4 teaspoon ground nutmeg
1/4 teaspoon ground cloves
2 apples, peeled & diced 1/2 to 3/4 inch
1/2 cup butter, room temperature
1 cup sugar
2 large eggs, beaten
2 teaspoons vanilla
1 cup buttermilk

1. Preheat the oven to 350°F and prepare a standard loaf pan with baking spray.
2. Combine the flour, cinnamon, baking powder, baking soda, salt, nutmeg, and cloves together in a bowl. Toss the diced apple into this dry mixture – this will help to keep the apple chunks suspended in the finished batter instead of sinking to the bottom.
3. Beat the butter and sugar together in a separate bowl. Add the eggs, vanilla and butter milk and mix thoroughly together.
4. Add the wet ingredients to the dry ingredients and mix until just combined. DO NOT OVERMIX. Place in the prepared loaf pan and bake for approximately 50 to 60 minutes, or until an inserted wooden skewer comes out clean.
5. Cool 5 minutes in the pan before removing to a wire rack to cool completely.

Makes 1 loaf

The World's Best Cornbread

"In my opinion, I am sure you have never tasted cornbread better than this!"

2 cups fine yellow cornmeal
1 cup all-purpose flour
2 teaspoons baking powder
1/2 teaspoon baking soda
4 tablespoons white sugar
2 cups grated cheddar cheese
2 cups frozen corn kernels
1 jalapeno pepper, diced small
1/2 red bell pepper, diced small
1 teaspoon salt
4 large eggs, beaten
1 cup sour cream
1 cup milk
1/2 cup vegetable oil

1. Preheat the oven to 400°F and spray a 9x13-inch cake pan with baking spray.
2. Place the cornmeal, flour, baking powder, baking soda, sugar, cheese, corn, jalapeno, bell pepper, and salt in a large bowl – mix to combine.
3. Place the eggs, sour cream, milk, and oil in a second bowl – mix to combine.
4. Add the wet ingredients to the dry ingredients and mix until just combined. Pour into the prepared pan and bake for approximately 30 minutes until golden brown and an inserted toothpick comes out clean.
5. Let cool in pan for at least 5-10 minutes, then cut into 12 to 24 equal portions.

Makes 12 to 24 portions

Yorkshire Pudding

Recipe Courtesy of BC Egg, BCegg.com

4 large eggs
1 cup whole milk
1 cup all-purpose flour
1 teaspoon salt
1/4 cup vegetable oil or beef drippings

1. Set a rack in upper third of oven and preheat oven to 425°F.
2. In a medium bowl, whisk together eggs, milk, flour, and salt until smooth. Set aside.
3. Place 1 teaspoon oil or beef drippings into each cup of a 12-cup muffin pan. Transfer pan to oven and heat until oil is smoking, about 2 minutes.
4. Remove pan from oven and quickly pour batter into cups, filling 2/3 full. Bake until puddings have risen and are golden brown, about 15 minutes. Serve immediately.

NOTES

To help ensure your Yorkshire puddings rise, avoid overfilling the tin. If you pour too much batter into each individual compartment, the pudding will begin to rise, but will then collapse because it is too heavy. To avoid this, only fill each compartment to be about 2/3 full.

Makes 12 portions

 Hens benefit from a balanced diet, just like us. Their feed is a blend of corn, wheat, soy (for protein), vitamins and minerals, and limestone for calcium.

RECIPE NOTES

PANCAKES & WAFFLES

Finnish Pannukakku (Finnish Oven Pancakes)

Recipe Courtesy of BC Egg, BCegg.com

3 teaspoons canola oil or vegetable oil
2 large eggs
1 tablespoon melted butter, cooled
3 tablespoons white sugar
1/4 teaspoon salt
2 cups milk
1 cup all-purpose flour
Toppings/Fillings (see "Notes" below)

1. Preheat oven to 400°F. Line bottoms and sides of two 15-inch x 10-inch (38 x 25 cm) rimmed baking sheets or jelly roll pans with aluminum foil. Brush foil well with oil using about 1-1/2 tsp (7 mL) per baking sheet. Place baking sheets in oven for 3 to 4 minutes just before adding pancake batter.
2. Beat eggs with electric mixer in large bowl until blended. Beat in butter, then sugar, salt, and milk. Add flour, beating well until blended.
3. Remove hot baking sheets from oven. Pour 1.5 cups egg mixture into each. Place baking sheets in oven. Bake until bubbles form and surface browns, about 20 minutes, switching position of pans in oven after 10 minutes.
4. Remove from oven. Bubbles will deflate. Starting at short end, roll up pancakes. Cut pancakes in half or slices to serve. Top as desired.

NOTES

If you only have one baking sheet, the recipe can be divided in half to serve 2 or bake the second pancake immediately after the first. Top or fill pancakes with any of the following options: slightly sweetened fresh or frozen (thawed) berries and vanilla yogurt; chocolate hazelnut spread, sliced bananas and chocolate syrup; sautéed sliced apples, ground cinnamon, sugar, and maple syrup.

Makes 4 portions

Blueberry Cheesecake Crêpes

"For breakfast or dessert — these crêpes are to die for!"

Cheesecake Filling & Cheesecake Sauce

1 cup cream cheese
1/2 cup ricotta cheese
Zest of 1 lemon finely chopped
Juice of 1/2 lemon
1 teaspoon vanilla extract
1 cup icing sugar, sifted
3 cups blueberries, divided

1. Stir the cream cheese until smooth and pliable. Stir in the ricotta. Add the lemon zest, lemon juice, vanilla and icing sugar. Blend until smooth.
2. Cheesecake Filling: use 1 cup of this cream cheese mixture combined with 2 cups of the blueberries.
3. Cheesecake Sauce: use the remaining cream cheese mixture combined with the 1 remaining cup of blueberries.
4. Refrigerate both bowls until thoroughly chilled.

Blueberry Topping

2 cups fresh or frozen blueberries
1/3 cup white sugar
Juice of 1 lemon
2 tablespoons apple juice, or cold water
1.5 tablespoons cornstarch
Pinch nutmeg

1. Combine blueberries, sugar and lemon juice in a pot over medium/high heat. Mash berries a little while cooking, for approximately 3 - 4 minutes.
2. Combine apple juice (or water) and cornstarch together in a small bowl and whisk into the boiling berry mixture. Stir until thick and remove from the heat. Stir in nutmeg.

Crêpe Batter

1/2 cup all-purpose flour
1/2 cup milk
1/4 cup lukewarm water
2 large eggs
2 tablespoons melted butter
1.5 tablespoons white sugar
Pinch of salt
Butter for the pan

1. Combine all the batter ingredients. Mix until smooth – a blender or food processor works perfectly. Place the batter in a container suitable for pouring. Cover and allow to rest for half an hour or refrigerate for up to 24 hours.
2. Place a non-stick pan over medium heat and coat with a bit of butter.
3. Stir the batter briefly. For each crêpe, pour about 2 - 3 tbsp of the batter into the hot pan – immediately lift the pan and start rolling the batter evenly over the pan surface. Cook until it is set and the bottom is golden before flipping it over to brown the other side.
4. Remove from the pan and continue cooking all your crepes- keep them stacked to keep warm.

To Assemble:

1. Spoon some of the cheesecake filling onto one side of a crêpe. Roll 1 to 3 of these crêpes per portion.
2. Spoon some of the cheesecake sauce over the crêpes, and then top with the blueberry topping.
3. Garnish with more fresh blueberries, powdered sugar, and a mint leaf if desired.

Makes approximately 8 crêpes

Fluffy Pancakes

Recipe Courtesy of BC Egg, bcegg.com

3/4 cup all-purpose flour
1/4 cup cornstarch
2 tablespoons wheat or oat bran or wheat germ, optional
1 tablespoon white sugar
1.5 teaspoons baking powder
1/2 teaspoon baking soda
1/4 teaspoon salt
2 large eggs
1 cup buttermilk or soured 2% milk*
2 tablespoons vegetable oil
1/2 teaspoon vanilla extract
Fresh berries or chopped fruit, optional
Maple syrup, optional

1. Stir flour, cornstarch, bran (if using), sugar, baking powder, baking soda and salt together in large bowl. Whisk eggs, milk, oil and vanilla in small bowl. Stir egg mixture into dry ingredients just until combined.
2. Spray large non-stick skillet with cooking spray. Heat over medium-high heat. Spoon about 1/4 cup batter per pancake into pan, spreading batter slightly. Cook until bubbles appear on surface, about 2 minutes. Turn and cook until lightly browned on second side, about 1 minute.
3. Serve immediately or keep warm while cooking remaining batter. Serve topped with fresh berries and syrup , if desired.

NOTES
To sour milk, pour 1 tablespoon vinegar into measuring cup; add enough milk to equal 1 cup.

Makes approximately 8 portions

Health Nut Pancakes

Recipe Courtesy of Katherine Desormeaux (Mrs. Chef Dez)

"Buttermilk has a thicker consistency, so if you choose to use skim milk instead you don't need as much"

1 cup whole wheat flour
1/4 cup wheat germ
1/4 cup ground almonds
2 tablespoons sesame seeds
2 tablespoons ground flax seed
2 tablespoons white sugar
1 tablespoon baking powder
1/2 teaspoon salt
1 large egg, beaten
2 cups buttermilk, or 1.5 cups skim milk
1 tablespoon canola oil (or extra virgin avocado oil)

1. Combine the flour, wheat germ, almonds, sesame seeds, flax, sugar, baking powder, and salt in a large mixing bowl.
2. In a separate smaller bowl, combine the egg, buttermilk, and canola oil together.
3. Preheat a non-stick pan or griddle over medium heat.
4. Pour the wet ingredients into the dry ingredients and mix until just combined – DO NOT OVERMIX.
5. With a large ladle, pour a portion of the batter onto the hot pan. Once bubbles form and start to pop on the surface of the pancakes, flip over to cook the other side until golden brown.

Makes approximately 8 to 10 four-inch pancakes.

Johnnycakes (cornmeal pancakes)

Recipe Courtesy of Katherine Desormeaux (Mrs. Chef Dez)

"My favourite pancakes!" ~ Chef Dez

1.5 cups whole wheat flour
1.5 cups cornmeal
3 tablespoons white sugar
1 tablespoon baking powder
3/4 teaspoon salt
2.25 to 2.5 cups buttermilk
3 tablespoons butter, melted
3 large eggs, beaten
3 tablespoons canola oil

1. Pre-heat griddle or large cast iron skillet over medium heat.
2. In a large bowl, whisk together the flour, cornmeal, sugar, baking powder, and salt.
3. In a separate bowl, whisk together the buttermilk, butter, and eggs.
4. Pour the wet ingredients into the dry ingredients and whisk just until smooth – do not overmix.
5. Brush some of the oil on the griddle/skillet. Pour batter 2 tablespoons at a time onto the griddle/skillet. Cook until the undersides are golden, about 2 minutes. Flip and cook 1 to 2 minutes more until both sides are golden. Transfer to a plate; keep warm. Repeat with remaining batter.

 No matter what type of eggs you buy, you're getting the same nutrients. Whether they're organic, free-range, free-run or your classic grocery store white eggs, they all have the same nutritional value.

Lemon Poppy Seed Pancakes

Recipe Courtesy of Chef Dez's Daughter Gianna, chefdez.com

"You can add syrup to these if you like, but I think they are best served with a sprinkle of sugar and a squeeze of fresh lemon"

2 cups all-purpose flour
1/4 cup white sugar
4 teaspoons baking soda
1.5 teaspoons salt
2 tablespoons poppy seeds
Finely grated lemon zest from 1 lemon
2 large eggs, beaten
2 cups milk
1 tablespoon melted butter
1/4 cup fresh lemon juice
Canola oil for the pan/griddle
Fresh lemon wedges for serving
More white sugar for serving

1. Pre-heat griddle, large cast iron skillet, or non-stick pan over medium heat.
2. In a mixing bowl, combine the flour, 1/4 cup white sugar, baking soda, salt, and poppy seeds together. Stir in the lemon zest.
3. In a separate mixing bowl, combine the beaten eggs, milk, and melted butter thoroughly together. Then stir in the lemon juice.
4. Combine the wet ingredients into the dry ingredients and mix until just combined. DO NOT OVER MIX.
5. Brush some of the oil on the griddle/skillet. Pour batter 1/4 cup at a time onto the griddle/skillet. Cook until the undersides are golden, about 2 minutes. Turn down the heat a little if needed. Flip and cook 1 to 2 minutes more until both sides are golden. Transfer to a plate; keep warm. Repeat with remaining batter.
6. Serve immediately with a squeeze of lemon and a sprinkle of white sugar on each pancake.

Makes approximately 20 four-inch pancakes

Pumpkin Spice Waffles

Recipe Courtesy of BC Egg, bcegg.com

"This recipe can also be used for pancakes! Just add a bit more milk to thin the batter to a more pancake-appropriate consistency, if needed."

2 cups all-purpose flour
1/4 cup white sugar
1 tablespoon ground cinnamon
2 teaspoons baking powder
1 teaspoon ground ginger
1 teaspoon ground nutmeg
1/2 teaspoon baking soda
3 large eggs
1.5 cups milk
3/4 cup canned pumpkin
2 tablespoons butter, melted
1/3 cup chopped pecans, toasted
1/2 cup maple syrup or table syrup

1. Preheat waffle iron. Combine flour, sugar, cinnamon, baking powder, ginger, nutmeg and baking soda in large bowl; mix well and set aside.
2. Whisk eggs, milk, pumpkin and butter in another large bowl. Stir in flour mixture until a slightly lumpy batter forms.
3. Spray waffle iron with cooking spray; add spoonful of batter and cook until waffles is set and golden brown, about 2 minutes. Keep warm while rest of batter is cooked. Serve waffles sprinkled with chopped pecans and drizzled with maple syrup.

Makes 8 portions

RECIPE NOTES

MISCELLANEOUS

Cloud Eggs

Recipe Courtesy of BC Egg, bcegg.com

"These fun and trendy eggs are the new craze on Instagram. Try them for your next brunch and you'll wow your guests."

4 large eggs
Pinch of salt
1/4 cup grated parmesan cheese
2 bacon slices, cooked and crumbled
1 tablespoon finely chopped fresh chives

1. Preheat oven to 425°F.
2. Separate eggs, placing egg whites into large bowl and each yolk into ramekin or small bowl.
3. Using an electric mixer, beat eggs whites and salt until stiff peaks form. Fold in cheese, bacon, and chives. Spoon into 4 mounds on parchment paper–lined baking sheet. Make deep well in centre of each mound.
4. Bake for 6 to 8 minutes or until golden brown and set.
5. Place egg yolk in each well and bake for another 3 to 5 minutes or until yolks are cooked to desired doneness.

Makes 4 portions

 The colour of an egg yolk is impacted by what a hen eats. If they have a diet rich in corn, the yolk will be much more golden than eggs from a hen who eats more wheat.

Easy Scrambled Eggs – makes 1 portion
Recipe Courtesy of BC Egg, bcegg.com

"Making scrambled eggs isn't complicated. A bit of salt and pepper for flavour, a little butter to cook, and fresh eggs is all you need for a perfect breakfast. You can modify this recipe to include your favourite ingredients such as cheese, salsa, vegetables, and herbs."

2 large eggs
Pinch of each salt & pepper
1 tablespoon butter

1. Whisk eggs, salt, and pepper in a small bowl. Melt butter in a non-stick skillet over medium heat.
2. Pour in egg mixture and reduce heat to medium-low. As the eggs begin to set, gently move a spatula across the bottom and sides of the skillet to form large, soft curds.
3. Cook until eggs are thickened, and no visible liquid egg remains, but the eggs are not dry.

Variations
Sprinkle eggs with grated cheese before serving, such as cheddar, Monterey Jack, or mozzarella. Fill a tortilla, toasted bagel, or English muffin for a quick and portable breakfast. Whisk in 2 tablespoons of milk for creamier eggs.

Egg Bread Boat
Recipe Courtesy of BC Egg, bcegg.com

1 pound (454g) French bread loaf
10 large eggs, beaten
1 cup chopped cooked bacon
1 medium red bell pepper, chopped (about 3/4 cup)
1/2 cup sliced green onions
2/3 cup whipping cream
1/2 teaspoon salt
1.5 cups grated cheddar or mozzarella, divided

1. Preheat oven to 350°F. Line a baking sheet with parchment paper. Using a serrated knife, cut a wedge into the top of the bread loaf cutting to about 1 inch from each long side. Use a spoon or your fingers to carefully remove the inside of the loaf, leaving about 3/4-inch shell. Place the bread shell on the prepared baking sheet.
2. In a mixing bowl, combine the eggs, cooked bacon, bell pepper, green onions, whipping cream, salt, and 1 cup of the cheese.
3. Carefully pour the egg mixture into the bread shell. Sprinkle with the remaining 1/2 cup cheese. Bake for 25 minutes or until eggs are set.
4. Let stand for 5 minutes. Using a serrated knife, carefully cut bread into slices and serve immediately.

Homemade Irish Cream Liqueur

"One may want to purchase pasteurized eggs in a carton if they are not comfortable consuming raw eggs in this recipe"

1.5 cups of Irish whiskey (or rye whiskey)
300ml can sweetened condensed milk
1 cup 10%MF cream
2 large eggs (or 1/2 cup of carton pasteurized eggs)
1 teaspoon instant coffee
1 teaspoon powdered chocolate drink mix, or chocolate syrup
1 teaspoon vanilla extract
Pinch of salt

1. Blend all ingredients together in a food processor or blender until completely smooth.
2. Dispense into sanitized bottles/lids. refrigerate immediately and consume within two weeks.

Makes approximately 4 cups

Hash Brown Egg Cups

"Tasty breakfast idea made from store-bought hash brown patties (60g each, measuring about 3 inches by 4 inches). Grate the cheese from a block for best results."

Butter (to grease the muffin tin)
6 frozen hash brown patties, thawed to room temperature
1/2 cup finely grated Parmesan cheese, divided
2 tablespoons drained, sliced, oil-packed sun-dried tomatoes
1 tablespoon minced onion
2 large eggs
1/2 teaspoon dried basil
1/2 teaspoon salt
A few grinds of black pepper

1. Preheat oven to 350°F Convection. If only doing a single recipe, then a toaster oven works great.
2. Grease 6 holes of a non-stick muffin tin with the butter.
3. Working carefully, press each thawed hash brown into each greased spot of the muffin tin, while making a "cup" shape (hash brown formed evenly over the bottom and the sides of each spot).
4. Bake in the pre-heated oven for 15 minutes.
5. Divide 1/4 cup of the grated parmesan equally into the bottom each hash brown cup and bake for another 5 minutes.
6. Equally divide the sun-dried tomatoes and onions into the cheese baked hash brown cups.
7. In a glass 2-cup measure, beat the eggs, with the dried basil, salt, and pepper until thoroughly combined. Pour this egg mixture evenly into the prepared hash brown cups. Top equally with the remaining 1/4 cup parmesan cheese and bake for another 15 minutes.
8. Let cool in pan for 5 minutes. Carefully remove each hash brown cup from the pan and serve immediately.

Makes 6 small portions

Homemade Eggnog

"The constant stirring of the egg mixture, while it is cooking, is vital to ensure that the eggs don't become scrambled eggs"

6 egg yolks
1/2 cup sugar
2 cups whipping cream, divided
1 cup milk (homogenized)
1/2 teaspoon ground nutmeg
Pinch of salt
1/2 cup dark rum or spiced rum
Fresh grated nutmeg, for garnish

1. In a stainless-steel bowl, whisk the egg yolks with the sugar until smooth.
2. Mix in the 1 cup of whipping cream, the milk, nutmeg, and salt until completely combined.
3. Place the bowl over a pot of simmering water. For a more temperate heat, make sure that the water does not touch the bottom of the bowl. Whisk the mixture constantly until it reaches a temperature of 160°F.
4. Remove the bowl from the heat and immediately chill uncovered in the refrigerator until cold.
5. While the mixture is cooling, whisk the remaining cup of whipping cream until soft peaks form.
6. Once the egg mixture is cold, fold in the whipped cream from the previous step.
7. Stir in the rum, pour into glasses and garnish with more freshly grated nutmeg.

Makes just over 5 cups

Italian Meringue

Recipe Courtesy of BC Egg, bcegg.com

"Italian meringue is used primarily as a cake frosting, but also forms the basis of divinity, mousse, and parfaits. It can also be used as a pie topping or be baked into hard meringues."

1 cup white sugar
1/3 cup water
4 egg whites
1/4 teaspoon cream of tartar

1. Combine sugar and water in small saucepan; bring to boil without stirring. Boil to soft ball stage (235°F (110°C), using a candy thermometer for accuracy. (Mixture will form a soft ball when small amount is dropped into cold water.) Use a wet pastry brush to brush down the sides of the pot, to avoid crystallization.
2. Beat egg whites in large bowl with electric mixer until frothy. Add cream of tartar and continue beating until soft peaks form.
3. Very slowly, while beating, pour hot syrup in very thin stream over beaten whites. Beat until whites are stiff and glossy.
4. Spread meringue over cake or pie and bake as directed.

Makes approximately 4 cups

Mushroom Omelet

"It is important to use strong cheddar as it adds more flavour. An omelet has never looked or tasted this good before!"

4 or 5 large button mushrooms, thinly sliced
4 teaspoons olive oil
1 tablespoon finely chopped onion
1 finely chopped garlic clove
2 large eggs, room temperature
1 tablespoon water

Salt and Pepper
3/4 cup grated old cheddar, loosely packed
Chopped parsley

1. Reserve four slices of mushrooms.
2. Put the remainder of the mushrooms in a pan with 3 teaspoons olive oil. Season with salt and pepper and cook over medium/high heat, stirring occasionally, until the liquid has evaporated, and they have browned. Remove from heat and set aside.
3. In a separate small nonstick frying pan over medium heat add 1 teaspoon olive oil. When the pan is warm add the four slices of raw mushrooms (from step 1), onion and garlic. Season with salt and pepper and cook until soft; approximately 1 to 2 minutes, stirring occasionally.
4. In a small bowl, beat eggs with water. Add to the onion, garlic, mushrooms in the small pan.
5. When the eggs begin to set around the edges use a heat resistant silicone spatula to loosen edges. Turn the pan while lifting the omelet to allow uncooked egg mixture to seep under the cooked egg.
6. Once almost fully set, turn heat to low and season with salt and pepper.
7. Place 1/4 cup of the cheese on half of the open omelet. Put 3/4 of the sautéed mushrooms (from step 2) on top of the cheese and put another 1/4 cup of cheese on top of the mushrooms.
8. With the silicone spatula fold the uncovered half of the omelet over the mushroom cheese mixture.
9. Layer on top of the omelet with half of the remaining cheese and then all of the remaining mushrooms and then the balance of the cheese. Leave omelet in the pan over low heat until the cheese on top is almost melted (covering with a lid or foil will help).
10. Carefully slide the omelet with the spatula onto a plate. Garnish with chopped parsley and enjoy!

Makes one large omelet.

Oatmeal Breakfast Bars – makes 16 portions

"The benefit of oatmeal in a convenient bar. Great for Breakfast on the run too – Microwave each bar from frozen for 30 seconds on high power."

2 & 1/4 cups whole wheat flour
2 & 1/4 cups quick oats
3/4 cup raisins
3 tablespoons ground flax seed
1.5 teaspoons baking soda
1.5 teaspoons ground cinnamon
1 teaspoon salt
3/4 cup butter, room temperature
1 cup dark brown sugar
1 cup unsweetened apple sauce
1.5 teaspoons vanilla extract
2 large eggs

1. Preheat oven to 350°F and prepare a 9x13-inch cake pan with baking spray. Tip: Line the pan with parchment paper leaving the ends sticking out to make the uncut product easier to remove from the pan once cooled.
2. Combine the whole wheat flour, quick oats, raisins, ground flax seed, baking soda, ground cinnamon, and salt in a large mixing bowl.
3. Beat the butter and brown sugar together in a separate bowl.
4. Add the apple sauce, vanilla extract, and eggs to the butter/brown sugar mixture. Continue beating until thoroughly combined.
5. Combine the mixtures in the two bowls together. It will be a very thick batter.
6. Press the mixture evenly into the prepared pan.
7. Bake for approximately 20 minutes until firm and the internal temperature reaches between 165°F and 170°F.
8. Cool completely in the pan until room temperature before cutting.
9. Remove from the pan by lifting with the parchment paper, and then cut into 16 equal sized bars. Wrap each bar individually with plastic wrap if freezing.

Spanish Omelet

Recipe Courtesy of BC Egg, bcegg.com

4 tablespoons olive oil, divided
4 Yukon gold potatoes, about 1 lb (454g), thinly sliced into 1/4-inch rounds
1 onion, very thinly sliced
1.25 teaspoons salt, divided
8 large eggs
1 teaspoon hot sauce
1/4 cup finely chopped fresh parsley
1/2 teaspoon ground black pepper
4 garlic cloves, minced
3/4 cup finely chopped red bell pepper

1. Heat 2 tablespoons of the oil in large non-stick or cast iron frying pan over medium heat. Add potatoes, onion and 3/4 teaspoon of the salt and sauté for 10 minutes, stirring occasionally.
2. Meanwhile whisk eggs, hot sauce, parsley, and remaining 1/2 teaspoons salt and pepper in medium bowl. Set aside.
3. After potatoes and onion have cooked for 10 minutes, add garlic and red pepper. Cook until potatoes are tender, and onions are lightly browned, about 5 minutes. Add potato mixture to the bowl with eggs. Stir to combine.
4. Heat remaining 2 tablespoons oil in the pan over medium-high heat. Add potato mixture and spread into an even layer. Cook until eggs start to set on the bottom, about 2 minutes. Reduce heat to medium-low. Cook until almost set, 8 to 10 minutes. Run a spatula around the edge and gently shake the pan to loosen the omelette.
5. Place a large plate over the pan. Carefully flip the pan over so the omelette falls onto the plate. Slide omelette back into pan. Cook until bottom is lightly browned, 5 to 7 minutes. Flip omelette onto plate and cut into wedges.

Makes 6 portions

Savoury Gouda French Toast – Makes 4 portions

"French toast doesn't always have to be sweet. This savoury application is perfect for any meal of the day, and even better with the fried egg on top! If you don't have Japanese mayonnaise, substitute with regular mayonnaise. If you don't like the spiciness of sriracha, then substitute with ketchup."

8 large eggs, divided
1/2 cup milk
1.25 cups grated smoked gouda, divided
1 tablespoon finely chopped fresh sage
2 teaspoons finely chopped fresh rosemary
1 garlic clove, minced
1 shallot, minced, approximately 2.5 tablespoons
1 teaspoon dry mustard
1 teaspoon salt
1/2 teaspoon ground black pepper
4 slices French bread, about 1-inch thick
2 tablespoons butter
Smoked paprika for sprinkling
Salt & pepper
Washed mixed greens for plating, optional
Japanese mayonnaise & sriracha, for garnish, optional

1. Beat 4 of the eggs thoroughly in a mixing bowl with the milk. Mix in 1/4 cup of the gouda along with the sage, rosemary, garlic, shallot, 1.5 teaspoons salt, dry mustard, and 1/2 teaspoon pepper. Transfer this to a shallow dish (like a 9x13 cake pan).
2. Soak both sides of the bread slices in the mixture until most of the liquid is absorbed, approximately 1 minute per side. Heat a large skillet over medium heat. Add the butter to melt.
3. Fry the bread slices on one side until nicely browned, approximately 3 minutes. While frying on this first side, spoon the remaining batter ingredients equally over the exposed top uncooked sides of the bread.
4. Carefully flip the bread slices over and cook the other side until nicely browned as well, approximately 3 minutes. Remove from the pan and place on a cutting board.

5. Set your oven to broil and prepare a baking sheet with parchment paper. Cut each cooked slice of bread in half on a 45-degree angle. Place the cut slices on the prepared baking sheet and top equally with the remaining 1 cup gouda. Lightly sprinkle with smoked paprika. Broil until the cheese has melted.
6. Fry the remaining 4 eggs to your liking and season with salt & pepper.
7. Plate each of the 4 portions as follows: Handful of mixed greens, 2 cut pieces of French toast (you have 8 pieces total to plate), 1 fried egg, and then drizzles of mayonnaise and sriracha. Serve immediately.

Spicy Fennel Nuts – Makes 3 cups

4 teaspoons fennel seeds
6 tablespoons white sugar
1.5 teaspoons salt
1 teaspoon ground cinnamon
1 teaspoon cayenne pepper
1 egg white
2 cups pecan halves
1 cup whole almonds

1. Preheat oven to 300°F.
2. Grind the fennel seeds in a mortal & pestle (or electric spice grinder)until mostly ground – they do not need to be completely ground into a fine powder.
3. Combine the ground fennel seeds with the sugar, salt, cinnamon and cayenne in a small bowl and set aside.
4. Whip the egg white to moist peaks in a large bowl.
5. Fold spice mixture into whipped egg white until thoroughly combined.
6. Add the pecans and almonds and gently mix together until the nuts are thoroughly coated, and then spread evenly over a large baking sheet.
7. Bake for 25 minutes. Halfway through the baking time, use a metal flipper to separate the nuts from the pan and redistribute the nuts.
8. Cool the cooked nut mixture on the pan until they are room temperature – the nuts will crisp up as they cool on the pan. Serve immediately or store in an air-tight container.

Western Omelet

"It is important to use strong cheddar as it adds more flavour. I use red bell pepper instead of the traditional green bell pepper. An omelet has never looked or tasted this good before!"

2 teaspoons canola oil, divided
1/3 cup 1/4-inch diced ham
1/3 cup small 1/4-inch diced red bell pepper
1 tablespoon minced onion
1 garlic clove, minced
Salt and Pepper
2 large eggs, room temperature
1 tablespoon water
3/4 cup grated old cheddar, loosely packed, divided
Chopped fresh parsley, for garnish

1. Put a small pan over medium/high heat. Add 1 teaspoon of the oil along with the ham and bell pepper. Cook, stirring occasionally, until the bell pepper is soft, and the ham is slightly browned, approximately 3 to 4 minutes. Remove from heat and set aside.
2. In a separate small 8-inch nonstick frying pan over medium heat and add the remaining 1 teaspoon canola oil. When the pan is warm add 1 tablespoon of the ham/pepper mixture from step 1, along with the onion and garlic. Season lightly with salt and pepper and cook until soft; approximately 1 to 2 minutes, stirring occasionally.
3. In a small bowl, beat eggs with water. Add to the onion, garlic, ham, & peppers in the small pan.
4. When the eggs begin to set around the edges use a heat resistant silicone spatula to loosen edges. Turn the pan while lifting the omelet to allow uncooked egg mixture to seep under the cooked egg.
5. Once almost fully set, turn heat to low and season lightly again with salt and pepper.
6. Place 1/4 cup of the cheese on half of the open omelet. Put 3/4 of the sautéed ham/peppers (from step 1) on top of the cheese and put another 1/4 cup of cheese on top of the ham/peppers.
7. With the silicone spatula fold the uncovered half of the omelet over the ham/pepper cheese mixture.

8. On top of the omelet place the remaining 1/4 cup cheese and then all of the remaining ham/peppers mixture. Leave omelet in the pan over low heat until the cheese on top is almost melted (covering with a lid or foil will help).
9. Carefully slide the omelet with the spatula onto a plate. Garnish with chopped parsley and enjoy!

Makes one 2-egg omelet

Toffee Meringue Kisses – Makes approximately 60 cookies
Recipe Courtesy of BC Egg, BCegg.com

6 egg whites, at room temperature
1/2 teaspoon cream of tartar
1.5 cups fine granulated white sugar
3/4 cup mini chocolate chips
3/4 cup chopped pecans
3/4 cup toffee bits
Cocoa, for dusting

1. Preheat oven to 250°F.
2. Beat egg whites and cream of tartar in large bowl with electric mixer until soft peaks form. Gradually beat in sugar by adding 1 tablespoon at a time, until sugar is dissolved and stiff, glossy peaks form. Gently fold in chocolate chips, pecans, and toffee bits all at once until well combined. Pipe or drop spoonfuls onto parchment-lined baking sheet. The cookies can be place fairly close together as they do not spread very much.
3. Bake for 35 to 40 minutes. If cookies start to brown, reduce heat to 225°F. Turn off oven and leave cookies to dry in oven with door slightly open for at least 2 hours.
4. Sprinkle cocoa through a sieve over cookies before serving.

NOTES
If you can't find fine granulated sugar, use food processor to grind regular granulated sugar to a fine powder. Or substitute granulated sugar.
When beating egg whites, to determine if sugar has dissolved, rub egg whites between your thumb and index finger; the mixture should not feel gritty.
If you don't have a piping bag, cut a 1-inch (1.5 cm) hole in the corner of a large Ziploc freezer bag, fill with cookie mix and gather at the top to form a piping bag. Cookies should be about 1 to 1-1/2 inches (2.5 to 4 cm) at the base.
Avoid making meringue cookies on a really humid day or they will be very sticky.

RECIPE NOTES

For more information on egg farming in BC, visit the BC Egg web page at BCEgg.com.

Egg Farming In BC

All BC egg farmers are inspected and audited regularly. In fact, the farmer's ability to house hens and sell their eggs relies on passing inspections and following the rules set by BC Egg to ensure the health and well-being of the hens and of the egg production system in BC. The system of supply management gives us a unique opportunity to be able to enforce standards of care consistently across BC in a way that wouldn't be possible otherwise. These standards of care are research based and evolve as we strive to learn more and continually improve egg farming in BC – for the hens, the farmers, and the consumers.

Healthy, Happy Hens

Our farmers pride themselves on not just meeting, but exceeding the animal care standards set for them. To keep their hens happy and healthy, farmers must manage a number of factors in their barns and on their farms.

Water – water goes through a filtration system so that the quality can be monitored easily. Vitamins and occasionally vaccines can also be added to the water system to ensure every bird receives a boost.

Food – hens have access to nutritious feed on a regular schedule. Bird weight and feed consumption are both monitored to ensure the hens aren't eating too much or too little.

Air quality – there are sensors in the barn to monitor air quality, and to alert the farmer if there are any problems. Barns have ventilation systems to keep fresh air flowing through and to keep dust levels under control.

Temperature control – barn temperature is always monitored to make sure the hens are cozy when it's cold and don't overheat when it's hot. Hens generate a lot of heat themselves, so cooling and ventilation are particularly important.

Manure Management – What goes in, must come out, and managing all the poop hens produce is an important part of keeping them healthy and the eggs clean. Each barn style has a different way of keeping the manure away from the hens, collecting it, keeping it dry, and moving it out of the barn. Chicken manure is a fantastic fertilizer so once it's collected from the barn, it's often used by crop or produce farmers. Fun fact: organic hens will produce organic manure!

Room to Move – Hens like to live in groups, called flocks, so it's natural for them to cluster together whether they're in a barn or out in a field. To ensure they still have room to exhibit their natural behaviours, the amount of space they have is regulated and there are limits on the number of birds that can be housed based on the size of a barn. Even outside space is regulated in free-range and organic fields.

Hen Feed: What's in it, and what's not?

Hen feed provides a complete meal with all the nutrients hens need to be healthy and to produce nutritious eggs. Their feed includes corn, wheat, fats, soybean meal (for protein), minerals (often in the form of limestone and salt), as well as enzymes, amino acids and vitamins that improve digestibility and round out the nutrition profile.

Two things you won't find in hen feed are hormones and steroids. These substances have been banned in Canada since the 1960s.

Antibiotics are another concern for many consumers but in egg farming they're very rarely required. Medically important antibiotics are only used when there are no other options and then only with veterinary supervision. If a hen receives treatment with antibiotics, her eggs are removed from production for the duration of her treatment. This way there's never any risk of eggs becoming contaminated with residual antibiotics and passing on to humans.

Eggs: The Right Choice

No matter what type of egg you buy, you're making the right choice. All eggs provide you with 6.5 grams of protein per large egg. Eggs also include 14 nutrients as well as all nine essential amino acids. Plus, they are very tasty and versatile. We hope you enjoy this cookbook and encourage you to cook with eggs more often.

INDEX

Bread, continued...

ABOUT THE AUTHOR

Chef Dez (Gordon Desormeaux) loves supporting BC Egg Farmers and he resides in the Fraser Valley of British Columbia, Canada with his family. His passion for food and people is second to none and anyone who has attended his live or online performances would agree.

Thousands have rekindled their romance for the culinary arts because of his infectious enthusiasm for bringing ingredients together.

www.chefdez.com